I'LL
WALK
AGAIN

I'LL WALK AGAIN

Andy Reinert and
Bink Burke

Burke Publishing   Chicago, IL

Cover & Design by Bernard Burke
Editing by Eileen Keeler and Kathleen Hodgman

This book was digitized via the Kurzweil scanner and typeset on Quadex 5000 and Compugraphic 8600 at Chicago Scan Typographers, Inc. a division of Bolchazy-Carducci Publishers, Inc.

Printed in the United States of America

First Printing, December 1986
Second Printing, September 1988
Third Printing, September 1991

International Standard Book Number
0-86516-183-6

Library of Congress Catalogue Number
86-72724

This book is dedicated to my brother,
John Joseph Burke, who helped me to
live with his love and laughter,
and helped me to die with dignity.

Andy Reinert

John

Andy

Laughter is the closest distance between
two people.

He, who has the courage
to laugh, is almost as much a master
of the world—
As he who is ready to die.

Gracomo Leopardi (Italian philosopher)

It has been said that by the time a person nears death the number of his friends can usually be counted on one hand. This has certainly not been true of Andy. As I began to list his friends and benefactors, I realized that this information would require not only the fingers of many hands, but also a great number of pages of this book. And there would still be the possibility that I would forget someone.

So I will simply say that Andy was very grateful for all that was done for him. The thousands of cards that were sent, the prayers that were offered, the many visits and phone calls, the generous donations of time and money were a tremendous source of strength and encouragement.

Through these kind acts Andy knew he had friends and how much he was loved.

I have heard you mentioned as a man whom everybody likes. I think life has little more to give.

Samuel Johnson

Contents

Foreword

*D*ear Bink and Family,

It was with great sorrow that Denise and I learned of Andy's death when we returned from our duties in California and to you and your family we offer our sympathy.

Andy was a young man that I counted as a privilege to get to know, and a young man whose courage and strength I will never forget. I appreciate so much being a friend of his and feel as though my life and ministry will be the stronger for it.

And yet it was not only the life Andy showed even in his pain that impressed me, but the strength and commitment of his family. Seeing the tremendous support network at work within your family was another thing I will not soon forget. The way you and your children consistently sacrificed your own interests in order to attend to the needs of Andy is truly worthy of praise.

Steve & Denise Schaick

Many people have remarked that it was unfortunate that such a gifted young man could not live to reach his full potential. The impact of this young boy's life, his outstanding courage in the face of death and tremendous pain and discomfort, his ability to conduct himself in such a selfless manner will remain in the memories of those who knew him and many who knew of him as an inspiration to face their own problems in the same manner. By his unusual example of human endurance, and the influence he had on the lives of others, Andy did reach his potential in his brief but heroic life.

Dr. Omer Renfrow
Superintendent
Evergreen Park High School

On June 16, 1983 after the funeral Mass for Nancy Tobin, a second grader from Most Holy Redeemer School, a telephone call came from the Archdiocesan Personnel Board. I received disappointing news that another priest was appointed to the Retreat House in Mundelein, Illinois. My hopes for continuing my ministry in a new challenge were shattered and I wondered why.

Early in August, 1984 the family of Andy Reinert phoned and asked if a priest could celebrate a Mass for him. He was in a coma and they believed he was dying. I celebrated the Liturgy with members of his family and friends who had gathered to pray for him.

Surprisingly, Andy pulled through the crisis and lived for almost another year.

I never had met Andy until that evening. After meeting him I visited him regularly. He never complained or even mentioned his long suffering hours of confinement. His beautiful spirit could not be crushed by his diseased body. I encountered a hero, and the courageous members of his dear family.

As time passed, I realized why I didn't become Director of the Retreat House. God wanted me to meet Andy and thru him, God wanted me to know that it was more important for me to continue my ministry as a parish priest. Thru Andy I received affirmation.

Rev. Michael J. Walsh
Holy Redeemer Parish

I remember Andy as a toddler—running around the neighborhood—usually chasing a dog or cat, (he really loved animals). I can remember his dark hair and big black eyes, and constant smile.

I got to know him better when he came up to summer camp in Owasippe to visit his brothers on family weekends.

I would be concerned because he would make a beeline for the lake. He loved to catch frogs, turtles and snakes.

It wasn't long before he was coming up to camp for the full two weeks as a scout himself. He attacked scouting and everything he did with the same enthusiasm as he did reptile catching and dog chasing.

He loved every aspect of scouting. He attended every meeting. If he missed one I would be concerned. He not only went on every 'overnight', he was usually the first one there, to help pack the equipment.

He advanced steadily and at the age of sixteen earned his Eagle rank—the highest rank in scouting.

Andy was a leader.

He was always offering new ideas on how to run the troop or a new place to camp on weekends.

Even when Andy became ill he still came to a meeting. His brothers brought him in his wheelchair.

Later, when he was confined to bed, and I would visit him at home, our conversation was dominated with scout activities—just completed or coming up. Even then he still offered suggestions. He never mentioned his pain or his illness.

Scouts like Andy don't happen every day. But when they do, they cannot be forgotten.

Andy was a dedicated person, he loved scouting—but more than that he loved life and people.

I'll remember Andy, and I'll miss him.

Bob O'Hara
Scout Master
Troop 608

Introduction

*A*ndy was the sixth son and twelfth child born to Bink Burke.

His Burke brothers and sisters had lost their father, Tom Burke, when he died suddenly from a heart attack.

After Tom's death, Bink married William Reinert, Andy's father. The marriage ended in divorce when Andy was not quite five years old.

Andy was showered with love, affection and a great deal of attention from his brothers and sisters. His brothers mentioned in this story are Tom, Mike, Dave, Bernie and John. His sisters are Eileen, Carol, Rosemary, Rita, Jeanne and Barbie.

Andy was a bright responsive baby. As a toddler he amused everyone with his quick laughter, and his unusual ability to understand. There was always one of his sisters or brothers to play with him and do things for him. Even though he was so often the center of attention, Andy never became "spoiled" as was predicted.

As Andy grew into his teens, he showed great promise of a wonderful future. He was ambitious, intelligent, handsome, good natured, and loved people.

When cancer struck suddenly, in the fall of 1983, both Andy and his family were stunned with disbelief.

At the time he became ill, he lived at home with his mother, and his brothers—Dave, Mike and John.

Andy had just entered his senior year at Evergreen Park High School. Dave and Mike were working. John was away at college. His other brothers and his sisters were married or living in their own homes.

They were all anxious to help in any way that they could.

But it was John who, realizing the seriousness of Andy's condition, insisted on quitting his last semester of college to stay with him. The tremendous patience and love that he showed towards his dying brother kept Andy's spirits high even in the face of unbearable pain and eventual death. Andy wrote about his feelings as he lay dying.

After his death, as his mother lovingly copied his last notes, she was inspired to finish his story.

Andy and Bink—Summer of 1968

Rosie's wedding, June, 1971
Front row—Eileen, Dave, Rosemary, Andy, Rita, and Bernie
Back row—Barbie, Carol, Bink, Jeanne and Mike

March, 1983
Andy earned his Eagle rank—the highest rank in scouting—
at the age of sixteen.

CHAPTER 1

Bad
News

When Grief gallops in on horseback,
Joy leaves—a step at a time.

Anonymous

I'm Andy. I'm seventeen years old. I have just been told that I have cancer, and that I will need a great deal of treatment. Also, they don't know when or if I will ever be able to walk again. I was alone in the room when they told me—except for Tim, my roommate. I'm scared, plenty scared.

I just called my Mom to tell her. She sounded plenty scared too. She said, "I'll be right there. Keep your chin up! We'll find a way." She made me feel a little better.

My back has been hurting since I fell when I was skiing with the Boy Scouts. I was going to a chiropractor for back treatments. It would seem O.K. for a while after he treated me, but then it would start hurting again. Yesterday he said that we had better check into the hospital to have tests made.

Last night was Halloween. My mom brought me in for the tests. I asked her to go through the local streets on the way so that we could see the kids in their costumes. We drove through the side streets. There were kids everywhere. We could hear them hollering "trick or treat."

Halloween was never one of my favorite holidays, but last night I would have given just about anything to be out there with all the kids—just to be walking.

We pulled up in front of the hospital. Slowly we made it to the front door. I am just really learning to use a crutch and my leg and hip were hurting so much.

Someone brought a wheelchair, and I tried to tell them it was O.K. I didn't need a wheelchair. But all of a sudden I was sitting in it and Mom was pushing me up to the desk marked "admittance."

The woman at the desk didn't smile, hardly even looked at us. The lights were glaring, and the whole place reminded me of the day I got my braces on. I glanced at the door through which we had entered, wishing we could leave. But we couldn't. We had to fill out all these forms and answer questions.

"We just came for some tests," my Mom told the lady. She made it sound like we wouldn't be staying long (I sure hoped not). Just find out what this is, and get me walking again.

I could see my mother's annoyance when the "frozen-faced" woman insisted on putting my name down as Andrew.

"His name is Andy," my mother insisted.

"His legal name?" The woman looked up for the first time.

My mother held her ground. I was admitted as Andy. That was good. I never did like being called Andrew.

After we filled out a couple of pages of questions, a nurse came to take me to my room. She pushed the wheelchair to the elevator. Up we went to Room 403.

I was happy to see a young person in the other bed.We were friends right from the start.

Pretty soon a nurse came into the room. She stuck an I.V. into my arm, inserted a catheter so that I could urinate—ug—that hurt. Then she gave me a shot in the shoulder.

"Why did I get a shot in the shoulder?" It's my leg and hip that hurt!"

The nurse laughed when I asked. "Doctor's orders," she said.

That's all I remember of last night. I must have fallen asleep from the shot.

I was awakened very early this morning. A sinister looking nurse was wrapping a tight rubber around my arm.

She jabbed a needle into my arm, emptied the catheter, and turned the light off. I could just barely see Tim's clock. It was not even five-thirty in the morning.

"Do they do this every morning?" I asked Tim.

"Oh yeah," he told me laughing. You'll get use to it. Tim went back to sleep.

I laid awake for a long time wondering what they were going to find wrong with me.

Just as I started to doze off, my breakfast arrived. It smelled so good. I could hardly wait to eat. I dug right in. Another nurse came in. She told me not to eat too much, as I would be going down for X-rays. I hurriedly ate everything on the plate. I was starving. To heck with the X-rays.

They took me down on the cart to the X-ray room. I laid there for a while until they finished. It didn't hurt, except for my back, which hurts all of the time. I waited a long time for a nurse to roll me back to my room.

Just after they helped me into my bed, Dr. N. came in. He stood at the foot of my bed and told me—that I have cancer.

CHAPTER 2

Testing

Tears sometimes weigh as much as words.

Ovid

*C*ANCER!!—I couldn't believe it, and they had told Andy while he was alone. I had to get to him fast.

I was shaking, when I finally arrived at the hospital. When I got up to Andy's room, however, I was surprised to find him in good spirits. He and Tim were laughing at a T.V. program.

I wasn't there long when the doctor came in to request a signature for a bone marrow test and a bone scan. Andy and I both signed the papers. Of course we had no idea of what this entailed. In a short time the doctor was back with a nurse. Time for the bone marrow test.

Andy was given a local anesthetic in the hip. He winced a little at that. But I'll never forget the absolute terror in his eyes when they took a piece of bone from his hip. He let out a holler that was almost animal like. I knew later that they had not even waited for the anesthetic to take effect. I had an immediate dislike for this almost inhuman doctor. So did Andy.

Shortly after that Andy was placed on a rolling cart to be taken for the bone scan. I accompanied him through the hall. I sat where I could watch through the large glass window. I could see Andy disappearing into the mouth-like opening of the mammoth machine.

There was a radiologist taking a reading from the ominous wavering lines appearing on the computer screen nearby. I kept thinking of scenes from the movie "Frankenstein."

I thought, "This is not real. This is not happening to Andy..." They soon had him back in his bed.

It was happening to Andy. It was happening to me too.

Andy was crying, and so was I.

He told me that the bone marrow test had been the most agonizing pain that he could possibly imagine. He said that it felt like a sledge hammer coming down on his hip, which hurt so badly anyway. They had also hurt his sore leg when they pushed it down to get him under the scanning machine. He was in terrible pain.

The two of us held hands and cried. I stayed with him until he fell asleep, and then I left for home.

The phone was ringing as I opened the front door. It was Dr. N. "You must be in the hospital at nine in the morning. We have decisions to make. Andy will need radiation, chemotherapy, and surgery. You did sign for surgery, didn't you?"

I could hardly answer him. He sounded more like he was trying to sell a refrigerator than talking about doing all of these things to Andy.

"I'll be at the hospital at nine," I told him.

Barb, Jeanne, Bernie and David were at the house shortly after I hung up the phone.

When I told them the terrifying news, they said that they wanted to go with me in the morning.

We knelt down together and prayed for help and guidance.

CHAPTER 3

Doctors
Doses
Decisions

*Eighteen times in every second a prescription
is filled by a white-coated pharmacist at one of
fifth-six thousand drugstores in the United States.
The staggering cost of these pink, violet, yellow,
white and green tablets, capsules, lozenges, and
amples amounts to over three billion a year.*

Marguerite Clark (Medicine Today—1960)

*I firmly believe that if the whole materia medica as
now used would be sunk to the bottom of the sea, it
would be all the better for mankind, and all the worse
for the fish.*

**Dr. Oliver Wendell Holmes (hailed as the most
successful combination the world has ever known
of physician and man of letters).**

*M*y decision was not made that night or the next morning. It had been made gradually over the past seventeen years. During that time the study of nutrition and its relation to health had become a daily part of my life.

I have said many times that if cancer struck myself or anyone in our family, I would not consent to the orthodox treatment of surgery, chemotherapy, or radiation.

These are my reasons: About eighteen years ago, I was in extremely poor health. I was always tired. I was suffering from severe sinus headaches. The black circles under my eyes reached to the end of my nose, and I was losing a great deal of weight.

It occurred to me that I might possibly have cancer or some other fatal disease.

Much as I dreaded it, I decided that I had best consult with a doctor. Doctors as a general rule have never been my favorite people. It has always seemed to me that they have an arrogance about them that is a barrier to most conversation. Certainly, the ratio of time that they have spent with me is not in proportion to the money I have spent with them. And I have found through trial and error that the majority of their remedies have proven useless. After finally forcing myself to call for an appointment, I was told that there would be a two week wait, because the doctor was out of town.

Two weeks later I arrived in the doctor's office at the appointed time. The waiting room was crowded. I found a chair and picked up a magazine.

Two hours and three magazines later my name was called. I was shown into an examining room where I waited another ten minutes until a nurse came in. She weighed me, took my blood pressure, listened to my heart, told me the doctor would be there in a few minutes. Another ten minutes passed before the doctor arrived.

"So you're tired, and you have a sinus problem?" he said after glancing at the nurse's notes.

Almost before I could answer, he was handing me a prescription which he said would probably help.

"However, we'd better check your blood, and make a few tests. You can go right into the lab, have these tests made, and come back next week."

With that he was gone. The nurse came in to ask me whether I cared to be billed or pay at the desk. I wrote her a check for twenty dollars and proceeded to the lab.

There was another 20-minute wait in the lab, and another bill. It was 5:30 when I left the doctor's office. I had spent three and a half hours of my time and thirty-five dollars of my money. The doctor had spent approximately three minutes with me.

The following week, I arrived one hour later than the appointed time. To my delight I only had to wait for one hour to see the doctor. The procedure was repeated, only this time I was given two prescriptions, and was sent to the lab for a basal metabolism test. This was a time consuming test. It was necessary to keep a mask over my face for about a half-hour which I found impossible to do. Consequently the test was inaccurate. The nurse told me that this sometimes happened. Regardless I was charged twenty-five dollars for it. I never did learn the results.

For approximately five weeks I continued to visit the doctor. There were more lab tests, a few x-rays, and more prescriptions. I was not feeling any better.

I did feel a little more relaxed, however, because I was now taking valium for a nervous problem— a side effect I had developed from the headache prescription.

The valium at least kept me from noticing how long I was in the waiting room. I could sleep until the nurse nudged me to let me know that they were calling my name.

CHAPTER 4

Health
Matters

Ye shall know the truth and the truth shall make you free.

(John VIII 32 c 115)

*I*t was in March of 1967 that I was introduced
to a whole new way of thinking. I was invited
to attend a meeting on the subject of "food
supplementation."

The gentleman, Gerry Wells, who spoke had been
formerly a minister. He was extremely sincere, and
quite knowledgeable. He told us the story of his
daughter: She had suffered from asthma since she
was a baby. They had gone to doctor after doctor in
search of help. They had tried every known remedy.
Eventually they moved to a warmer, and drier
climate. They had been told that her problem might
possibly be caused by the inclement weather in the
Midwest. Her condition only worsened, as they
continued to seek help. Gerry and his wife, Betty,
would not give up, even though they were watching
their bank account shrink, (they had already spent
over seven thousand dollars).

At the suggestion of a friend, Gerry started to give
his daughter a "food supplement." He was ready to
try anything.

Within a few months, his daughter began to show
improvement. Her lungs began to clear, and she

began to play and run without choking up. It wasn't long before her health was almost completely restored.

Gerry and Betty were amazed and delighted. Gerry was anxious to tell other people about this wonderful supplement. And so his career with Don Hillestad, President of the Hilcoa company began.

Gerry started out as a salesman. It wasn't long before his unusual ability to speak on the subject of nutrition found Gerry travelling all over the United States and later into other countries. He had an exciting story to tell the world. And Gerry told it better than anyone I have ever heard.

He offered a simple way of protecting health in this concentrated food supplement formulated by Don Hillestad.

That night Gerry told us what had happened to our food in the past twenty years, and why such "foodless" food was causing so many health problems.

Gerry told us this simple story about what has happened to our food:

> Man has so tampered with our foods either by food-robbery or adulteration that the eating of these deficient foods may bring us many health problems. There is mounting evidence that Civilization has tricked us!
>
> WHEAT STORY: Whole wheat provides many nutritive elements for the health of the body. The life-factors are carefully preserved by Nature, with a coating which keeps them sealed in and ready to be used

when this seal is broken. Kernels of wheat have kept as long as 6,000 years. Some have been found in Egyptian pyramids which were put in there many years ago, but when they are planted, they GROW!

SOIL ANALYSTS tell us that 25 years ago, they tested wheat off of a certain piece of Kansas soil and found it to measure from 20-30% protein. Now, it measures from 7-11% protein, so even when we get it in the best state possible it is still inferior to what it was 25 years ago. The miller refines and processes our grains to get white flour that will keep for years. No vermin will eat it because it has been robbed of its life-giving properties. To make white flour, the protective hull is broken first.

1. The bran is removed, which takes from it all the minerals which are so vital to health.

2. The middlings, tailings and shorts are all removed, as worms and weevils and bugs still like the product and are attracted to the life in it. If there weren't life values present, they wouldn't be interested!

3. The wheat Germ, the heart of the wheat, is taken out also. When the heart of any living thing is removed it is DEAD, DEAD, DEAD! Not even a dumb insect would have it with the LIFE all gone, but WE eat it by the ton in America. (30% of our diet is made up of white flour products.) Value? you guessed it! ZERO!

4. The Wheat Germ oil is removed, along with the germ. This could cause flour to become rancid if it sat on the shelf long, so the oil is taken out, along with 25 lipids, so vital to health. This oil is also rich in natural Vitamin E, the heart and muscle vitamin. Now there is NO NATURAL FORM of this vitamin left! (One nutritionist said you'd have to eat 256 slices of white bread to ever get enough of your MDR of Vitamin E.)

5. The end result: White devitalized, bleached, enriched (?) flour. All 25 lipids, plus approximately 25 vitamins, minerals, and amino acids are removed and the miller adds back 4 or 5 synthetics, man-made imitations of the REAL thing and calls it ENRICHED! Are you enriched, or are you ROBBED?

(Cows fed refined—degermed—grain died of heart failure! Of a herd of 28 fine cattle, 13 dropped dead in 3 years when fed the refined grain so universally used by people in our country.)

Sugar story: Raw sugar is loaded with minerals; the very thing our bodies are starving for and remember that vitamins without minerals are USELESS AS SAWDUST. Processing removes the blackstrap molasses so that the product won't be sticky, and, along with this go the minerals, which are later added to the cows' hay and the pigs' food. (Calcium, phosphorus, iron, thiamin, riboflavin, etc.) We get the left overs! Refined white sugar—a foodless food, with NO value whatsoever to HEALTH. Many experts feel that it is the cause of many modern-day diseases! (20% of our national diet consists of white sugar! Value? Again—NONE.)

Rice Story: The brown rice has supported life in the Oriental countries for years, but WE want rice that cooks in 5 minutes so off goes the hull and with IT many valuable nutrients. This is given to animals in feed supplements, and WE get the left-overs—again!

We take a supplement simply to add back all these stolen factors to the devitalized product, in order to regain something of what is lost from its original state. We CANNOT expect health from deficient foods!

To maintain ANY measure of health in its most vibrant state, we MUST do something to make up for these losses!

Gerry held up a box of the concentrated food supplement. He explained that the little tablets in the box contained all the vitamins and minerals that we must have daily to keep our bodies functioning at top level.

The integrity and honesty of Gerry and the people I met that night, left no doubt in my mind that what he was saying was the truth.

I went home with my first package of Hilcoa tablets. I could hardly wait to try them. I was tired of waiting for doctors. I was tired of buying expensive prescriptions. I was tired of being sick and tired. I wanted to feel better.

After just a few weeks of taking the little golden tablets, I began to feel terrific. I could hardly believe it. I was full of energy. The circles under my eyes were fading. My sinus problem cleared up. My headaches had ceased. And best of all I stopped taking the prescriptions.

I cancelled my next appointment with the doctor.

I began to give the tablets to Andy who was one year old at the time. He was suffering from a severe asthmatic condition. In a few months Andy's asthma was under control, with only a few flare-ups. Until now that was the only severe illness that Andy had ever experienced.

With great enthusiasm I began to give them to the other children. They, too, experienced new energy and more resistance to the "common cold," and other such problems.

We were using so many of the wonderful little tablets, and everyone I told about them wanted to try them. I began to sell them. I thought this would at least pay for what we were using. It was exciting and rewarding to have people call for more, and tell me that they too were feeling better.

Health stores became my hang out as I searched through their books for information on nutrition. I read everything I could find on health and diet. I attended every nutritional seminar possible that this wonderful company offered. I met people from every city in the United States, from every occupation. They were farmers and bankers, salesmen and secretaries, athletes and doctors, men and women— young and old. They came with their families, their neighbors and their friends.

They told unsolicited stories about how they had tried physicians and surgeons, hospitals and medications, tests and pills. Rarely did any doctor suggest that they might need a better diet.

In the majority of cases they were not only made to feel worse, but developed new problems from the side effects of the heavy medication and sometimes radical surgery which they had received as routine treatment for their problems.

After taking the nourishing tablets, they too noticed a tremendous improvement in their health, and energy.

CHAPTER 5

Cancer Cures— To Be— Or Not To Be

God, give us men!
A time like this demands
Strong minds, great hearts, true faith
and open minds.
Men who possess opinions and a will,
Men who have honor;
Men who will not lie.

*T*hrough my many new friends in the health food business I met a group called International Association of Cancer Victims and Friends. I became a regular subscriber to their journal.

The following information has been copied from the journal:

Dr. Jones, physiologist with the University Dept. of Medical Physics, has been studying cancer for more than 23 years. These are some of the things he said in 1974:

> "Beyond the shadow of a doubt, radical surgery on cancer patients does more harm than good.
>
> Chemotherapy does nothing to prolong a patient's life.
>
> As for radiation treatment—most of the time it makes no difference whether the machine is turned on or not.
>
> These cures are worse than the disease."

NBC's "FIRST TUESDAY" TV PROGRAM

The cancer segment of NBC's "First Tuesday" TV program on March 2 was a disappointment to most of our members.

The first part of the program was fairly objective with interviews with Dr. Contreras, Laetrile patient Robert Klein, Hoxsey patients, other Laetrile patients, and interviews with Ernst Krebs, Jeannie Glickman of our Long Island Chapter, and Norman Fritz.

Then Robert Klein's doctor from Stanford, Dr. Jesse Steinfeld, Surgeon General, and Dr. Charles Edwards head of the FDA, proceeded to dismiss Laetrile as having no value. Hoxsey, Gerson, or any of the other non-toxic therapies were called quack treatments.

The accuracy of these spokesmen seems to be on a par with the total amount of their clinical experience with Laetrile, Hoxsey, Gerson, or any of the other non-toxic therapies—nothing.

Then NBC's reporter stated that Laetrile was of no value and that there was no scientific evidence to support its use.

NBC had refused to interview several previously terminal patients who were willing to be interviewed. They also refused to interview Dr. Burk—the most highly placed scientific proponent of Laetrile in the U.S. His statements would have offset the views of Steinfeld and Edwards who seemed to parrot the views of organized medicine.

The Stanford spokesman and NBC did not mention that the Stanford doctor had written a letter nearly five years before giving Robert Klein only a very short time to live, or that he had been so weak he had to be carried to Dr. Contreras' office.

In the program NBC refused to state the city where they filmed IACVF. For a time they would not give the location to anyone who called or wrote for IACVF information, directing them instead to the American Cancer Society. They later changed this policy after most of the inquiries ceased.

As a result, IACVF received only a few inquiries instead of thousands.

A number of people wrote letters to NBC objecting to the manner of presentation. Our attorney requested an opportunity for a factual response based on the fairness doctrine. NBC replied that it is illegal to treat cancer with Laetrile in the U.S., therefore the fairness doctrine does not apply.

The program did have some merit in that millions of people were at least exposed to the non-toxic therapies who otherwise might never have heard of them.

The following letter to NBC was a superb effort of research and reporting on the many aspects of Laetrile by David Martin, a staff member of a U.S. senate committee.

Mr. David Martin
Bowie, Maryland 20715
March 9, 1971

Mr. Julian Goodman
President, NBC
30 Rockefeller Plaza
New York, N.Y. 10020

Dear Mr. Goodman:

I was one of the millions of viewers who watched your First Tuesday presentation of March 2 dealing with unorthodox cancer therapies and cancer clinics in Tijuana. I was profoundly disappointed, and more than a little angry.

I had a very direct interest in your program, especially in the portion that dealt with Laetrile. This interest stemmed in the first place from the fact that my wife has an inoperable cancer and that we had turned to Laetrile because orthodox therapy offered so little hope. And my interest was accentuated by the fact that I was in Tijuana when Mr. Delaney and the NBC crew filmed their sequence of Dr. Contreras, and I visited Dr. Krebs and Mr. McNaughton in San Francisco after the San Francisco sequences had been filmed.

I want to enter the strongest possible protest against the bias that was evident throughout the presentation, against the inexplicably inadequate research. On top of this, perhaps I have had somewhat more motivation than Mr. Delaney to do an intensive job of research on the validity of the claims that have been made for Laetrile. After all, my wife's life was at stake. But the lack of comparable motivation still does not excuse Mr. Delaney and NBC. For the fact is that there is a mass of evidence—not "single shreds of evidence" supporting the thesis that Laetrile treatment is often effective in the treatment or palliation of cancer, and particularly effective in eliminating or reducing the agonizing pains that are characteristic of terminal cancer.

Laetrile may be controversial. But any honest presentation of the subject should at least make clear the fact that the advocates of Laetrile include a number of outstanding medical men and scientists in the world—in Germany, in Italy, in the Phillippines, in Canada, in Mexico, in Belgium and in the United States. Not only did the presentation ignore this essential and easily ascertainable information, but it assured your audience in categorical terms that Laetrile is rejected out of hand by the entire U.S. medical profession.

Ninety-five percent or more of the United States medical profession did not even know that Laetrile existed—until your "First Tuesday" program brought it to their attention. (My wife's oncologist, a man of outstanding reputation, told us that he had never heard of Laetrile when we informed him that we were leaving for Tijuana). Certain moguls of the AMA and of the 'cancer establishment' within the AMA are opposed to Laetrile, as I soon discovered from several contacts with cancer experts. On the other hand, roughly two hundred American doctors who were themselves victims of cancer have come to Dr. Contreras for treatment when orthodox therapy offered them no hope. Moreover, had Mr. Delaney taken the trouble, as I did, to check through conscientiously the six volumes of the McNaughton Foundation's application to the Food and Drug Administration, he would have discovered that American medical men of the very first rank were open-minded enough about Laetrile to be willing to use it experimentally and to participate in the work of monitoring and evaluating the results. The pharmacological monitor named in the application, for example, was Dr. Chauncey D. Leake, a man who has served as President of the American Association for the Advancement of Science, President of the American Society for Pharmacology, and President of the Society for Experimental Biology and Medicine.

There are three categories of proof of the validity of Laetrile therapy which should have been available to the NBC researchers had they made a serious effort to be objective.

First, there are the results of animal efficacy experiments.

Second, there are the reports of a number of outstanding medical researchers in other countries—and in the United States—who have worked with Laetrile over the past 20 years.

Third, there are the records of case histories of the hundreds of Americans who have benefited from Laetrile therapy, administered in this country as well as in Mexico and Germany. Let me deal with these proofs in the order listed above.

1. THE ANIMAL EFFICACY EXPERIMENTS:

The application submitted by the McNaughton Foundation to the Food and Drug Administration contains, as one item, the results of a large scale experiment conducted with four hundred rats by Bioresearch Laboratories Ltd. of Canada. In these experiments, the two hundred cancerous rats in the control group received no Laetrile; the other two hundred rats received systematic injections of Laetrile. On the average, the rats who received Laetrile survived 80 per cent longer that those that did not.

It can be argued with some validity that drugs that are effective in treatment of diseases in rats will not necessarily have the same effect in the treatment of the same disease in human beings. What cannot be argued at this point is that Laetrile has no effect on cancer in rats.

2. THE REPORTS OF MEDICAL RESEARCHERS:

Even if there had been no massive experience internationally with the use of Laetrile in human cancers, the very impressive results achieved in the tests conducted with rats would certainly suggest the advisability of using Laetrile experimentally in human beings, perhaps on terminal cancer patients initially. But the fact is that there now exists an international roster of some 5,000 cancer patients who have been treated with Laetrile. The records or case histories are there, and the files are open.

(1) Dr. Hans A. Nieper: In their current application to the FDA for a permit to use Laetrile experimentally, the McNaughton Foundation includes a letter dated January 2, 1972, from Dr. Hans A. Nieper, Director of the Department of Medicine at the Silbersee Hospital in Hanover, Germany, and one of Germany's foremost cancer experts. Dr. Nieper earlier helped to develop Cyclophosphamide and other drugs now used in the treatment of cancer. This is what he had to say on the subject of his experimental use of Laetrile:

"We have now treated some 70 patients and I can say that the treatment of cancer and of chronic meyloid leukemia (the worst form of leukemia—D.M.) with Laetrile is, on the average, by far more beneficial than any other treatment we have so far applied and of which we are aware. It is especially superior to Cyclophosphamide and to the antimetabolites. We have observed with Laetrile, regressions of histologically confirmed tumors and metastases which we have documented. There is an improvement in the general condition of the patients in almost all cases. Most convincing is the effect of Laetrile in patients suffering from Myeloid leukemia. Three of these came in terminal condition after treatment with Myleran, X-ray to the spleen and Cyclophosphamide proved to be unsuccessful. These patients are now back in their professions, feel practically healthy, and their spleen has regressed by some 70% in volume."

Dr. Nieper's enthusiasm for Laetrile might be suspect if he himself were the developer of Laetrile or a prime mover in its use in cancer therapy. If this were the case, those who are disposed to be suspicious could accuse Dr. Nieper of touting his own product. But Dr. Nieper had nothing to do with the development of

Laetrile nor can he even claim to be among the early pioneers, in the application of Laetrile therapy.

As he points out in his letter, he first heard about the use of Laetrile in the treatment of cancer at the 9th International Cancer Congress in Tokyo in 1966. He was impressed by what he heard—and curious, as a scientist ought to be. And as soon as he returned to Hanover he began to work with Laetrile.

The paragraphs that have been quoted above summarize his basic findings—findings which are all the more impressive because they come from a man who has worked broadly with the entire spectrum of cancer therapies.

Dr. Nieper's experience parallels the independent experiences of an impressively long list of researchers in the United States and internationally.

(2) Dr. Ettore Guidetti: One of the earliest Laetrile pioneers was Professor Ettore Guidetti of the University of Turin Medical School. In July of 1954, Dr. Guidetti reported to a conference of the International Union Against Cancer in Brazil that he had administered Laetrile to a series of patients suffering from terminal cancers of the uterus, cervix and rectum and with ulcerating breast cancers, and that the treatment had brought about destruction of the cancerous tissue. He also reported that, after giving Laetrile to patients with lung cancer, he had been "able to observe, with the aid of radiography, a regression of the neoplasm or the metastases."

When an American doctor, after Guidetti's presentation, rose to inform the conference that Laetrile had been investigated in the United States and had been found worthless, Dr. Guidetti replied, "I do not care what was determined in the United States. I am merely reporting what I saw in my own clinic."

(3) Dr. Manuel D. Navarro: In the Phillippines, Laetrile therapy has been used with marked success for

some fifteen years now by Dr. Manuel D. Navarro, Professor of Medicine, at the University of Santo Tomas, an internationally distinguished researcher who has more than 100 major scientific papers to his credit.

Dr. Navarro said in his letter of January 8, 1971 to Mr. McNaughton:

"I...have specialized in oncology for the past eighteen years. For the same number of years I have been using Laetrile in the treatment of my cancer patients. During this eighteen-year period I have treated a total of over five hundred patients with Laetrile by various routes of administration, including the oral and I.V. The majority of my patients receiving Laetrile have been in a terminal state when treatment with this material commenced. It is my carefully considered clinical judgment, as a practicing oncologist and researcher in this field, that I have obtained most significant and encouraging results with the use of Laetrile in the treatment of terminal cancer patients and that these results are comparable or superior to the results I have obtained with the use of the more toxic standard cytotoxic agents."

(4) Dr. N. R. Bouziane: In Canada, Dr. Nieper's experience had been anticipated by the earlier experience of Dr. N. R. Bouziane, Director of Research Laboratories and Chemotherapy Specialist at the Hospital Ste. Jeanne d'Arc in Montreal. Professor Bouziane, like Dr. Nieper, is a scientist of international reputation. Among other things, he has served as Dean of the American College of Bioanalysts. After treating a score of cases in the late 50's Dr. Bouziane reported:

"In our investigation, some terminal cases were so hopeless that they did not even receive what we consider the basic dose of 30 grams. Most of the cases, however, became ambulatory and some have in this short time resumed their normal activities on a maintenance dosage."

(5) Dr. Ernesto Contreras: Although there is a disposition to treat Tijuana doctors as quacks, the fact is that Dr. Ernesto Contreras is one of Mexico's most distinguished medical researchers. He did part of his postgraduate training at Harvard's Children's Hospital in Boston, an institution which has an unsurpassed qualitative reputation, and he subsequently served as Chief Pathologist at the Mexican Army Hospital in Mexico City, and as Professor of Histology and Pathology at the Mexican Army Medical School. In his letter of January 16th to Mr. McNaughton, Dr. Contreras summarized his Laetrile experience as follows:

"Since July 1963 until now, I have tried Laetrile as a palliative agent, in several hundreds of terminal cancers, the majority of them after having tried all the approved methods.

The palliative action is effective in about 60% of the cases. Frequently, enough to be significant, I see arrest of the disease or even regression in some 15% of the very advanced cases.

I have found Laetrile to be absolutely non-toxic in the recommended therapeutic doses, even when administered for periods over six months continuously. I have used it intrarterially, intravenously, intracavitary and orally with excellent tolerance."

The list of foreign specialists who have worked with Laetrile and have been impressed by the results they have achieved now includes several score men in more than a dozen countries. I remain open to correction, but I have thus far heard of no foreign medical or scientific researcher who has worked with Laetrile and who has turned his back on it or has failed to be favorably impressed by the accomplishments it made possible. The results warrant all the more credibility because all of these researchers have worked independently and have no vested personal interest in proving Laetrile either effective or ineffective.

When the FDA says that there is no clinical evidence to support the claims made for Laetrile, or when Mr. Delaney parroting some of the completely close-minded medical criticism of Laetrile, informs the American people that 'there is not a shred of scientific evidence' that Laetrile is effective in the treatment of cancer, they are, in effect, saying that all of the eminent foreign medical men I have named are charlatans or quacks. It would be more becoming on the part of both FDA and Mr. Delaney if they tackled the issue frontally instead of implication, and said in so many words that Dr. Nieper, Professor Navarro, Professor Guidetti and Dr. Bouziane and all the others are charlatans whose scientific evaluations are— worthless —because if FDA and Mr. Delaney were to make this assertion, they would then be confronted with the legal as well as scientific responsibility of providing proof for their assertions.

In the preceding paragraphs I mentioned the 1953 report of the California Cancer Commission. This item deserves a few paragraphs of attention because the 1953 California tests are repeatedly invoked by the opponents of Laetrile.

At the urging of Dr. Arthur Harris, an early Laetrile practitioner, the California Cancer Commission in 1952 agreed to use Laetrile experimentally on a number of terminal cancer patients. Laetrile was administered to 41 patients, all of them hopelessly terminal. The total amount given to each patient ranged from 50 to 100 milligrams—compared with the daily dose of 6, 000 to 9, 000 milligrams used in recent years by Laetrile practitioners. The report of the Commission found that there had been no objective improvement in the condition of the patients. But it did concede that there had been a noticeable 'subjective improvement'—that many patients suffered less pain, that they felt better and ate better, and even put on weight.

Next to the gift of life itself, there is no more precious gift that any medication can offer on a terminal cancer patient then relief from pain. If this is all that Laetrile accomplishes, it would still constitute more than ample justification for the use of Laetrile in cancer therapy—and I am certain that 99 percent of the American people would concur with this estimate on a simple common sense basis.

3. SOME REPRESENTATIVE CASE HISTORIES

No solid judgment can be made on the basis of a single experience—and on this point I note that your presentation created the impression that the case for Laetrile rested largely on the claimed improvement of one young man, Mr. Robert Klein. With minimal effort for a large organization it would have been possible to locate a hundred cancer patients who have been considered terminal cases before receiving Laetrile, and who are today alive and well. It should have been possible not only to interview the patients themselves, but to interview the doctors who have treated them, both prior to and subsequent to Laetrile therapy, and to check the hospital records. The application of the McNaughton Foundation to the Food and Drug Administration, contained as exhibit 10 detailed and documented case histories of cancer patients in the Los Angeles area who had been treated with Laetrile by Dr. Maurice Kowan. Two or three days of leg work should have been sufficient to check out all of these cases. Although, with a sick wife, my time was limited, I did check on a number of them. I find it difficult to understand why NBC, with all of its resources, apparently failed to check with any of them.

One of Dr. Kowan's more remarkable cases was Mrs. S.G., age 70. In January, 1968 she had undergone an exploratory operation at St. Vincent's Hospital in Los Angeles. The operation revealed that she was suffering from cancer of the cecum, with generalized metastasis involving the liver and intestines. A bypass was performed in her intestines, but the cancer could not be removed. She was declared to be in a hopeless terminal condition, with a life expectancy of months only.

When Mrs. G. first came to see Dr. Kowan at the end of March 1969, she was suffering from continuing nausea and abdominal pain, had marked jaundice, and had a hard nodule mass in her upper abdomen, involving the liver area. She was immediately put on daily treatments of Laetrile.

In early July, because she was still suffering from abdominal distress, Mrs. G. went back to St. Vincent's Hospital for another exploratory operation. The operation revealed multiple gallstones—which were removed—but it also revealed no trace of cancer or the presence of any tumorous mass. A biopsy was negative for malignancy.

When I spoke to Mrs. G. within the past week, she informed me that she was still in good health and had returned to work as a practicing attorney.

Another of Dr. Kowan's cases I spoke to was Mrs. K.W. In 1966, she developed a tumor on her larynx. The tumor was removed surgically on February 1, 1967, but the operation revealed an infiltrating squamous cell carcinoma, Grade 11 to 111. The pathologist's report read: "Examination of the biopsies of the vocal cord shows them all to be replaced by an invasive squamous cell carcinoma."

When Mrs. W. first came to Dr. Kowan in February 1967 she was unable to swallow food except in liquid form and was unable to speak above a slight whisper.

She was so weak that she found it extremely difficult to get out of bed in the morning. Because she did not want to tell her oncologist that she was receiving Laetrile treatments, she submitted to 40 cobalt treatments at Cedar Hospital during February and March 1967 at the same time as she was receiving Laetrile injections.

She responded very rapidly to treatment, recovering her voice and her ability to eat solid food. Her voice today is strong, her health is good—and there is absolutely no sign of cancer. Her oncologist—who does not know of the Laetrile treatment to this day—has said to her repeatedly: "It's amazing—I just can't believe my own eyes. It's a miracle." The oncologist could not believe his eyes because the complete disappearance of this kind of cancer just doesn't happen with cobalt therapy.

Mrs. W. is convinced from her immediate positive reactions to Laetrile injections that she owes her recovery and her life to Dr. Kowan and Laetrile.

Dr. Kowan's case histories deserve the most careful attention and scrutiny from the medical profession. Because he complemented his Laetrile therapy with a rigid dietary regime and detoxification program, he achieved results which, qualitively and percentagewise, surpass the already favorable results achieved by other Laetrile practitioners. For example, in treating approximately one hundred cancer cases, most of them terminal, he was able to achieve dramatic relief from pain in virtually every single case. (I have been able to check personally with only a few of Dr. Kowan's ex-patients, but it should be a relatively simple task for a medical commission, or for that matter, for any enterprising reporter to check with the several score people who, thanks to Dr. Kowan, are still alive and in good health today, after being given terminal warnings by their physicians years ago.)

As a parenthetical tribute to Dr. Kowan I think it proper to include the information that the several patients with whom I spoke all told me that the fees Dr. Kowan charged for his therapy were ridiculously low by general standards.

It is a sad commentary on the blind unreasoning opposition of the medical establishment that Dr. Kowan, after a trial that should rank in history with the Scopes Trial, was sentenced to 30 days in the workhouse for using Laetrile—which was described in the testimony as "a worthless drug" by no less a person than Dr. Jesse Steinfeld, the present Surgeon General.

Much more remarkable was a case of a woman we came to know well while we were in Tijuana. Just over three years ago, she had had a hysterectomy, followed by 31 cobalt treatments. Last October she developed cancer of the spine. Within a matter of weeks she was paralyzed from the waist down, unable to move a toe, and without control of her bowels or bladder. Her husband brought her from Kansas wearing diapers and in a wheelchair. After five days of Laetrile injections she could not only move her toes but could raise her knees waist-high in bed. She had also regained control of her bladder. After ten days, she stood erect for the first time in months. I spoke to Mrs. R.R. only a few days ago and she informed me that she was still doing well and was trying to teach herself to walk with the aid of a walker.

I might also mention the case of Mrs. H.M., another Kansas resident, who was accommodated in the room next to ours. Mrs. M. had a highly advanced case of intestinal cancer and was in terminal condition at the point of arriving in Tijuana. Her husband told me that her pain had been so intense that she had repeatedly begged him to let her die. It was questionable from the beginning that Laetrile could save her life. But at least the Laetrile injections did give her dramatic relief from pain. Although there were times when she still suffered much discomfort, she was able to sit up and chat with her neighbors or play cards with her husband, and sometimes she even went to the beach with him. Life, at least, had been made bearable for her—and for this her husband was infinitely grateful.

It may be possible to argue about one case, like that of the Klein boy, that Laetrile had nothing to do with the dramatic improvement in the patient's condition, that it was due either to a spontaneous remission or to previous therapy. But at the point where one has to account for 20 or 30 or a hundred cases that have improved spectacularly and immediately, or almost immediately, after receiving Laetrile injections, then common sense suggests the existence of a pattern that simply cannot be explained on the basis of spontaneous remission or by reference to previous therapy. And these overly facile explanations become even more inadequate if it can be demonstrated that Laetrile brings significant or dramatic relief from pain in the overwhelming majority of cases.

So much for Mr. Delaney's categorical assertion that there is not "a shred of scientific evidence" that Laetrile is beneficial in the treatment of cancer.

I am sure that Mr. Delaney was told by a number of ranking cancer experts that Laetrile was worthless. In this respect, his experience would parallel my own. For example, before we left for Tijuana my brother-in-law insisted that I call a Baltimore cancer expert to obtain his opinion of Laetrile therapy. I had just been to see Dr. Dean Burk, head of the Cytological Chemistry Division at the National Cancer Institute, NIH, a biochemist of international reputation who had been the recipient of several awards for research in cancer. I had been greatly impressed by Dr. Burk's affirmative evaluation of Laetrile therapy (a) because he had used Laetrile for several years in extensive experiments with animals, (b) because he had taken the trouble to visit Dr. Contreras in Mexico, Dr. Nieper in Germany, and Dr. Guidetti in Italy to study the experience with Laetrile therapy in these countries. On the basis of my reading and a four hour meeting with Dean Burk, I was already leaning heavily in the direction of Laetrile. But since my brother-in-law wanted me to get another evaluation, I agreed to remain open-minded until I had spoken to the Baltimore cancer expert.

The cancer expert in question, as I had anticipated, told me that Laetrile was "sugar pills." Had he told me that he had used Laetrile experimentally on X number of patients and found it completely ineffective, I might have been impressed. But when I asked him whether he had ever used it himself, he said that he had not. When I asked him whether he had ever travelled abroad to study the experience with Laetrile therapy in Germany, Italy, Mexico, the Phillippines or other countries, he replied that he had not. And when I asked him if he had ever made a first hand study of the pros and cons of the subject, again he conceded that he had not. He was simply repeating what he had heard from others who, in their turn, were probably repeating what they had heard from others, going all the way to the antiquated 1953 report of the California Cancer Commission.

I must say that I was singularly unimpressed by what the Baltimore cancer expert had to tell me.

Mr. Delaney informed your audience that the Food and Drug Administration would refuse to approve Laetrile for experimental use. Since the FDA had only a few days previously received the McNaughton Foundation's 6 volume application for a permit to use Laetrile experimentally, I simply cannot believe that FDA had already examined the application, decided against it, authorized Mr. Delaney to say that the application would not be approved. Until it is demonstrated otherwise, I prefer to believe that the FDA will examine this application in a conscientious and open-minded manner, in keeping with its charter and its responsibility to Congress and to the American people.

Nor am I prepared to damn the handful of powerful men in the medical establishment who up until now have been fighting the war against Laetrile with the obdurate fervor of crusaders. They are, after all, not only doctors, but human beings. And it is almost certainly because of the general weakness that the medical profession historically has always offered resistance to new therapies and ideas, before taking them up. Harvey, Lister, Pasteur, and a host of other medical pioneers all ran into this kind of resistance from their peers.

I know how difficult it is for any man in public life to reopen his mind once he has committed himself to a position. But it is still my hope that, in the light of the growing volume of foreign testimony, the handful of influential medical men who have thus far been blocking the experimental use of Laetrile will reconsider their position. They are prepared to concede that Laetrile, even in large doses, is harmless. Why not, then, agree to the experimental use of Laetrile—under properly controlled conditions—on terminal patients for whom orthodox therapies offer no hope?

If the tests do in fact prove that Laetrile is worthless, their opposition to date will be vindicated. And if the tests demonstrate that Laetrile has merit, they would be able to take credit for this finding, too, on the basis of their open-minded agreement to permit the testing to proceed.

Conversely, history will judge them harshly if they persist in their opposition to testing, and if the weight of evidence from the continuing use of Laetrile in other countries finally overwhelms them and compels its acceptance in the United States. For, with or without their assent, Laetrile will continue to be used by ranking medical men in other countries. The A.M.A. can slow down the process because of its enormous influence in world medicine, but they cannot stop it.

It was my hope that NBC would make an open-minded presentation and then conclude with an appeal for an open-minded attitude. I was profoundly disappointed on both scores.

I shall be happy to cooperate with NBC and Mr. Delaney in any future presentation on the subject.

Sincerely,
David Martin

Copy to: Accuracy in Media &
each U.S. Senator

CHAPTER 6

Dr. Harold Manner

The simplest and most necessary truths are always the last believed.

John Ruskin (Modern Painters 1856)

*I*t was in 1975 that I read about Dr. Harold Manner. Dr. Manner was a teacher and biochemist at Loyola University. He became interested in information that he was reading about Laetrile in the cure of cancer. Believing that it could not possibly be of any great value, he and his class of young students at Loyola began to experiment with groups of mice.

Three groups of mice were injected with cancer cells. The first group were given chemotherapy, and orthodox treatment. They lost the hair on their bodies, lost their appetites and were dead in a short time.

The second group was given Laetrile and their regular diet. They suffered less pain, did not lose their hair and lived slightly longer.

The third group was given Laetrile and massive doses of minerals and vitamins. They recovered completely in six weeks time.

Through these tests he realized that Laetrile without the support of a good diet and mega doses of vitamins, minerals and enzymes was useless.

But he discovered that Laetrile combined with a good diet and massive doses of vitamins and minerals could actually destroy cancer cells and restore health.

Dr. Manner and his students were amazed and excited about this new discovery. They contacted the news media and medical doctors with the wonderful results of their experiment. At first the news media gave him very favorable coverage. He appeared on many radio and T.V. programs.

Manner wanted to learn more about the use of Laetrile and other cancer cures. He travelled to Mexico and to Europe to meet with many of the doctors mentioned in Dave Martin's letter. Once while in Mexico he said he was appalled by the attitude of our American doctors. Some of their comments were:

"This couldn't possibly work."

"What do these people know? After all we have studied medicine. We have degrees."

"Certainly we have greater facilities and knowledge than they do."

European doctors seemed to have a more open mind. They wanted to learn everything they possibly could. They, too, had watched many people suffer and die with cancer. If there was anyway of helping these people they wanted to know about it.

Was it possible that the real cure was in this simple change in the body's internal environment and not in the X-ray machines and powerful drugs?

Dr. Manner continued to study their methods, and conduct his own experiments. He established a Laetrile clinic in Glenwood. People were coming to him from every city. Most of them had tried the "orthodox" methods and only found themselves growing worse from the insidious side effects of these expensive treatments that rarely saved lives.

The news media and the AMA began to harrass him. He was even threatened with arrest if he continued to treat people with this "quack" treatment as they liked to call it...this in spite of the fact that some terminal patients were recovering—and even those who could not be saved were spending their "last days" without pain or indignity.

I attended several of Dr. Manner's lectures. I observed that he really believed in what he taught. He was interested in helping people—not just in making money.

Because of his beliefs he left his teaching position at Loyola. His new thinking was not in accordance with the "system." His clinic in Glenwood was forced to close.

This could not stop this man from carrying out what he believed to be the truth.

As many before him he took his treatment outside of the United States. He set up a clinic in the West Indies on the Island of Montserrat.

I had followed his career closely in the newspaper, and eventually in the Cancer News Journal. I had frequently said over the past years that Dr. Manner would be the one I would call if the need ever arose.

His home phone number was still in my book. I dialed his number. His wife answered the phone. She told me that he was in Oregon, and she expected a call from him within the next hour. She would ask him to call me.

The call came that night as we knelt praying for guidance. Dr. Manner's voice sounded so reassuring. I told him of Andy's condition.

He told me of some of the success treatments that they had been having. He said he thought that they could help Andy. He gave me a number to call in Florida to arrange an immediate flight.

The decision was made. This method offered Andy more of a chance with much less suffering than anything offered in our hospitals here. With these convictions I was prepared to meet with the doctors in the morning. It was a long sleepless night as I pondered over what was ahead of us.

We arrived in the hospital a little before nine the next morning, so that we could have time to talk with Andy before meeting with the doctors. When we told Andy that we had made the decision to take him to the West Indies for treatment, he looked as jubilant as a prisoner who was suddenly told he would be freed.

"When do we go?" Andy asked.

"Just as soon as we can arrange a flight—probably Monday," I told him.

"That's great—I can hardly believe it. Oh, Mom, that's really great. You always did believe in Dr. Manner's treatment. Wow, imagine—the West Indies—get me some maps. How far is it?"

I tried to impress Andy with the importance of secrecy. He couldn't understand why anyone would try to stop us.

We met with the doctors around a conference table—Jeanne, Dave, Barbie, Bernie, and myself. They gave Andy's cancer a name. He had Ewing's Sarcoma, a fatal cancer that would grow swiftly. They had never known it to be cured. There was a large tumor in his left pelvic area which would eventually cause complete paralysis and death. They recommended immediate treatment of chemotherapy followed by surgery and radiation. The treatment would be long and painful. Without this treatment Andy could not live.

"And with the treatment," I asked, "what are his chances?"

"With the treatment he would have a 2% chance," we were told.

We got up from the table and said that we would have to consult with Andy.

Andy was in great spirits at the prospect of leaving the hospital and going to the West Indies.

His brothers and sisters had gathered around his bed. They were laughing and playing card games with him. The happy atmosphere must have mystified the doctors and nurses in attendance. They were not aware of our plan.

Dr. N., the little Indian doctor who had originally given Andy the news while he was alone, came in and stood at the foot of the bed. (This is the spot they all choose for their sixty dollar visits, if they come to the side of the bed—this is called an intense visit—the charge is greater).

He said, "Andy, you're going to have chemotherapy, surgery, and radiation." He actually clapped his hands (I almost expected him to jump up and down).

I, too, was standing at the foot of Andy's bed. Before he could advance to the more expensive spot on the side of Andy's bed, I looked him in the eyes and said, "We'll be leaving here—we're seeking another opinion."

His face fell. He turned and walked out of the room. That was the last time that we ever saw him.

We didn't want the hospital to know that we were taking Andy out of the country. He was still only seventeen. I was afraid that if they found out they might try to stop us.

I remembered the story of little Chad Green, whose parents had been ordered by the courts to continue him on chemotherapy. They were threatened with arrest and imprisonment because they had "smuggled" their son out of the country, for a treatment that they believed would give him a better quality of life. They had seen how much worse he had become after the dreaded poisonous drugs had been administered.

It took us until the next day to get everything together. Dave rented a wheelchair. He and John went to the hospital to pick up Andy the next evening.

They brought Andy home with all of his records and X-rays. With great anticipation we prepared to leave the country.

CHAPTER 7

We Leave For Montserrat

If a man does not keep pace with his companions, perhaps it is because he hears a different drummer. Let him step to the music which he hears, however measured or far away.

Henry David Thoreau (Walden)

We left the house at 5:30 a.m. in order to get to the airport in plenty of time. Dave, Jeanne, Barbie, and Bernie were with us. Andy wanted to ride in the back of Jeanne's wagon so that he could rest as much as possible. He was happy and excited about the trip, but still in a great deal of pain. He insisted on carrying the bottle of "pain-killers" in his pocket. He wasn't taking any chances that I would lose them.

Even though we thought we had given ourselves more than enough time, we just barely made our flight. Things go slowly, when you are travelling with a wheelchair, pillows, crutches, and all the paraphernalia that was necessary for Andy's comfort.

Andy tried to help from his wheelchair by carrying whatever he could handle. It was so strange to be waiting on Andy. He had always been so independent, and capable of doing everything for himself.

Jeanne and Dave boarded the plane to help us to our seats. As they were asked to leave, I realized how much we were going to miss them. Their faces looked sad. Andy's fate was uncertain, and we would be far away. Even a letter would take a week or more to reach them.

But the excitement of the flight soon put all other thoughts out of our minds. Andy was so glad to be out of the hospital, and he hadn't been on a plane since he was a baby. His smiling face revealed the happiness he felt in the anticipation of our journey.

We were scheduled to land in Miami, change planes to Antiqua, and then to connect with our final flight to Montserrat. Fortunately we were met in Miami by two representatives from the clinic. There was only a half-hour between connections. The airport was crowded and confusing. Also, (remembering the story of little Chad Green) I was worried that we might be stopped for seeking Laetrile treatment for a minor outside of the United States.

The girl at the ticket office did ask for a medical certificate, when she saw Andy in a wheelchair. The representative from the clinic, however, did all the talking and soon had us on the plane to Antiqua.

I breathed a sign of relief when the plane took off. We were out of the U.S. Andy could have the Laetrile treatment. No one could stop us now.

About three hours later—at almost 5 p.m.— we were landing on the island of Antiqua in the West Indies.

Andy didn't seem to be in much pain any more. (I found out later that he had taken seven Demerol tablets during the trip).

We met others in the Antiqua airport who were travelling to the clinic. There was Carol Brown, a medical technician, and Crystal, a 75 year old lady.

Crystal had breast cancer and had tried other treatments—unsuccessfully. She felt that the clinic offered her some hope.

In spite of the difference in their ages she and Andy were soon carrying on a lively conversation.

We didn't have too long to wait in Antiqua, until it was time to board the twelve passenger plane that made one flight daily to Montserrat. Andy needed help getting on. There were steep stairs to climb. He was lifted by two handsome young natives. They were so healthy looking and friendly. Their big smiles made it easy to talk with them. They spoke perfect English, and sometimes—to each other— what they called—"chit-chat". It sounded a little like "pig-latin"—set to music.

One of the young men who had helped lift Andy onto the plane was the pilot. He invited Andy to sit next to him. Andy happily consented.

The trip from Antiqua was a thriller. We flew low over the Caribbean. The pilot pointed out the other islands. We were flying so low that we could see people on the ships below, and even see the ripples in the vast waters.

As we approached Montserrat, the pilot warned us that we would feel as though we were flying right into a mountain. I held my breath as we dropped swiftly on to a very small landing strip.

I was watching Andy's face as we landed. He was thoroughly enjoying himself, and so was the pilot. They were busily talking. Andy was pointing towards the approaching mountain, (probably instructing the pilot on how to land, I thought to myself).

We landed safely. We didn't hit the mountain.

The bus from the clinic met us at the tiny airport. We drove leisurely through the scenic little island. We were on the last mile of our long journey.

CHAPTER 8

Welcome To Paradise

A Prayer in Darkness

Thank God the stars are set beyond
my power,
If I must travail in a night of wrath;
Thank God my tears will never vex a moth,
Nor any curse of mine cut down
a flower.
Men say the sun was darkened: yet I had
thought
it beat brightly—even on calvary:
And He that hung upon the Torturing Tree
Heard all the crickets
singing, and was glad.

*W*hen we arrived at the clinic, Andy was
disappointed in the number of stairs—and
no ramps or elevators. He knew that it would be
difficult for him to get around on his own.

In his typical fashion, he expressed his disappointment, and proceeded to make other plans. By the time
we reached our room, he had already asked the two
young men who had helped him down the stairs if
they would be available to help him when he needed
them. They assured him that they would be at his
service any time he called. And they were.

Our room was simple and pleasant. Large picture
windows overlooked the sloping lawn. The lawn
contained many tropical plants. There were flowers
everywhere. In the distance we could see the ocean.

We would share the same room for our three week
stay. Dr. Manner believed that having a relative with
each patient was an important part of the cure. He
also knew that we would learn more about their
treatment. That way we could carry it on when we
were ready to return home.

As we settled ourselves, we could hear this funny
little singing of what sounded like crickets. We found
out later that they were small frogs, about the size

of a quarter. They would cling to the leaves of the surrounding bushes, start their song at sundown, and sing until dawn. They seemed extremely noisy that first night. But after a few nights, we hardly noticed them.

Andy fell asleep early. I'm sure it had to be the effect of the seven Demerol tablets he had taken on the plane.

When I was certain that Andy was sound asleep, I ventured out into the hall. Next to our room was the nurses' station. Further down the hall was a huge dining room, where the patients, doctors, nurses, staff, and some medical students from a nearby school, had their meals.

The dining room had one open wall. Beyond the wall was an olympic-size pool. It was on the top of an incline.

I walked out and stood at the edge of the pool. There was no one around. I could see the Caribbean waters stretching out in every direction until they met the dark sky. The moon was full and cast its reflection on the water. The brilliant array of stars sparkled like diamonds against the contrasting darkness. It was truly a tropical paradise.

All of this beauty, however, just emphazied my heavy heart and loneliness. I thought of the words of a song, "Why has such beauty lost its splendor? Is it because I'm losing you?"

I went down on my knees and started to cry. "Dear God," I prayed, "please help Andy to get well and to walk again." I thought of the suffering that he had already endured, and the uncertain days ahead. As I knelt there, I suddenly felt a hand on my shoulder. It was one of the nurses.

"Don't cry, dear," she said. "God loves you and your son. He will help you."

We prayed together for a few minutes. Her name was Edith—a very dear and dedicated nurse, whom we grew to know and love.

She walked back to the room with me.

Andy was still sleeping.

I fell asleep in the bed next to his—listening to the strange sound of the singing frogs.

CHAPTER 9

Getting
Acquainted

There are no more important ingredients of a properly constituted diet than fruits and vegetables, for they contain vitamins of every class, recognized and unrecognized.

Henry G. Bieler, M.D.
(Food Is Your Best Medicine)

*O*ur first morning at the clinic, a doctor and nurse came into the room to explain to us how they hoped to heal Andy. They told us of the high percentage of recovery they had achieved with terminal patients.

They outlined their plan as follows:

(1) There would be an intensive detoxification program to eliminate toxins that interfered with body functions. This would be accomplished with a juice fast for two days, and coffee enemas every evening.

(2) An intensive nutrition program would provide all of the raw materials his body needed.

(3) Laetrile and D.M.S.O. would be given along with massive doses of Vitamin C. to destroy the malignant cells without damaging normal cells. These would be given daily through I.V.'s.

(4) Numerous vitamins and enzymes would be given to Andy every hour. These were to build up the immune system, (the lymph glands, thymus, and spleen) to produce the T. cells necessary to fight the cancer.

It certainly made a great deal more sense than shooting the poisonous chemotherapy drugs into his already diseased system.

The first two days in Montserrat were lonely. We were almost 4000 miles away from home. Somewhere along the way, all of our luggage had been lost. It contained not just our clothes, but many books and games, which we had hoped would occupy our time.

We weren't very well acquainted yet. We were pretty much confined to the room. Andy was still in such pain that he did not care to travel around in his wheelchair.

So except for the hourly arrival of our tall glasses of a combination of carrot, lettuce and celery juice, varied only with taller glasses of beet juice, there was little we could do.

We did a great deal of talking to each other during this time. Andy talked about going back to camp and wondered how long it would be before he could finish school. He wanted badly to graduate with his class.

He talked about some of the things that he had done, that he thought were really bad, and he felt sorry about.

They didn't sound very wicked to me. I assured him that I had done far worse things. He laughed and agreed with me—pointing out many of my faults and mistakes.

I never felt that Andy was criticizing me when he reviewed my bad habits. I rather enjoyed it. It was the way that he would put it. He knew me well. And I knew him just as well. He'd always tell me that I was improving. It was more like a father talking to a daughter, than a son talking to a mother.

Of course, Andy had to play his little tricks on me. One night he had asked Kim, one of the younger nurses, to place a rubber tarantula in my bed. I didn't see it right away. Just before I got in bed, Andy asked for water. I brought him a pitcher of fresh water. As I was about to turn the light off, I saw the threatening creature. It looked so real with its fuzzy back, skinny legs and beady eyes.

The nurses had told us that there were spiders and snakes in the surrounding area. I thought one of the group had invaded our room.

I stood looking at it for a minute, and then let out a scream. There were several nurses in the hall (they knew what Andy was up to). They were waiting for the fun. I didn't disappoint them.

I opened the door and hollered, "Help me, there's a tarantula on my bed."

By that time Andy was laughing hysterically, and so were the nurses.

Andy said, "Mom, didn't you know it was a fake spider?"

The "fake spider" became a nice conversation piece, as well as the beginning of some close friendships.

The patients began coming in to find out what was causing so much amusement.

As they came into our room, they introduced themselves. There were only about five patients in the clinic—each was accompanied by a relative. They had all been diagnosed as "terminal." They had all received radiation, chemotherapy, or surgery—one or all types of treatment. They all agreed that it had done them more harm than good.

There was Diane—a young mother of three children. She had had chemo and surgery. She suffered from breast cancer. She recovered somewhat during her stay. She died the day before Christmas seven weeks later. She and her mother-in-law were from Connecticut.

Melissa came into the room. She was ten years old travelling with her mother. Melissa had been operated on for a brain tumor. She made a good recovery while at the clinic, but died about six months later. Their home was in Pennsylvania. She came in every day after that to talk with Andy.

There was Crystal, whom we had met in the airport. She was travelling alone. Crystal is still living. She resides in California.

We did not meet Doug that night. Doug's cancer was similar to Andy's—only much more advanced. He had not been able to walk since his arrival the week previous to ours. He was 52 years old. He lived in Colorado. Doug died a few months later.

We were from every part of the United States. Our backgrounds were different. Yet we had so much in common.

We had all come for the same reason: to find a cure for cancer.

CHAPTER 10

In Everything Give Thanks

Now thank we all our God,
With heart, and hand and voices
Who wondrous things hath done
In whom his world rejoices.

(Catherine Winkworth 1648)

*A*fter the first two days of fasting, we were able to eat again. Our food consisted of salads with very little dressing, (usually just safflower oil and lemon). Raw cabbage and carrots were a daily "treat". Muffins and breads were made fresh from whole grains. Either millet or oatmeal was served every morning. Fresh fruits and vegetables (most of these were grown on the island or shipped from close by) were served in abundance. There were no poisonous sprays used. There was freshly caught fish, fresh chicken and turkey.

Forbidden foods were white sugar, red meats, canned foods, white flour, and no foods containing artificial additives such as flavoring, colorings, or preservatives. Snacks of fruit and of course our vegetable juices were available at all times.

The hourly packages of vitamins, enzymes, and minerals were distributed every day by the nurses.

Each afternoon the I.V.'s were administered.

During the first week Andy experienced a few setbacks in his progress. He had headaches, chills, and stomachaches. These lasted only a short time, however. The doctor said it was a normal reaction to the detoxification.

By this time we had become well acquainted. There was such a positive happy atmosphere at the clinic. There were frequent visits from the other patients and their relatives. The doctors and nurses spent much time with us. They were gentle, efficient, and informative. There was no feeling of rushing through every conversation.

Everyone loved Andy. They were amazed at his calmness, his consideration for the other patients and those who cared for him, and most of all his unceasing cheerfulness, which made it a pleasure to be with him.

Things were surely looking better—our luggage had been found! It arrived on the strong shoulders of a smiling young bus boy. When we asked him his name, his smile broadened.

"My name is Abraham Lincoln."

He helped Andy to unpack his box of games and books. He appeared as excited as Andy as they viewed the recovered treasures.

Young Abe came in often after that to learn to play some of the games that Andy had brought. He told Andy many stories of his activities on the island. He tried to teach Andy how to speak the native "chit-chat." Andy loved to listen to him, but declined to learn.

"I'll stick to English," Andy told him.

But whichever language they spoke, Abe and Andy understood each other. Their friendship grew strong in spite of the difference in their culture.

Yvonne, the physical therapist, came mornings and evenings to work on Andy's legs. (Yvonne had been trained in England, and lived on a nearby island with her doctor husband).

Her methods were quite different from the ones that I have observed being used here. She worked on the muscles and nerves. There was no manipulation of the joints, as I have watched physical therapists do in our hospitals here.

Andy felt greatly relieved after her 45 minute treatments.

At this point they were able to remove the catheter that bothered him physically and emotionally.

When Yvonne arrived for therapy the following morning, Andy announced that he was going to the "whirlpool" with the other patients. Yvonne was delighted. She had been coaxing him to try it.

The "whirlpool" was a huge tub located on the beach. The tub was filled with hot mineral water twice a day. The water came from a nearby mountain stream. Patients and relatives would submerge themselves in the swirling waters. After this they would go into the clear cold tub, which was next to the hot one.

Everyone clapped when they saw Andy approaching. He was the last one in as he had to walk so much slower. His walking had improved a great deal, though he was still using one crutch.

From that day on, Andy went down to the tubs twice a day. Yvonne worked on his leg muscles while he was in the hot water.

After several days of this treatment, I noticed that he was no longer in pain! He didn't need any pain killer. We were extremely excited about that. The treatment was working!

He began to eat his meals next to the swimming pool.

No longer were we eating alone in our room.

He was soon able to swim a little in the pool. It was wonderful to see him swimming, even though he couldn't get enough movement in his legs to swim as well as he had. That worried Andy. (He had always been such an excellent swimmer).

"I've got to be able to swim, and get back to camp by July," he told Yvonne.

"You will," she promised. "I know you will."

Finally there was news from home. One day as Andy sat by the pool, he was handed three packages, and many cards and letters from the family and friends. He was happy and excited to be so well remembered.

Andy continued to feel better and was enjoying the warm weather and breath taking environment. The days were passing swiftly. We were now in the last week of our stay. We would be leaving that Saturday—November 28th.

Thursday was Thanksgiving. Thanksgiving is not a celebrated holiday in the West Indies. But these wonderful people knew it was of great significance to all of us homesick Americans.

Fay, the nutritionist, had brought us a card inviting us to the dining room on the night of Thanksgiving. She had planned a special dinner.

Fay's holiday dinner will always be remembered. We sat together at one long table. It was covered with a white cloth. The table was set with beautiful china and silver. There were lighted candles at each end of the table. There were fifteen "guests." Even Doug had managed to join us.

The dinner was nearly a traditional one, and yet it was different. The turkey had never been frozen. The dressing was made from corn bread. The vegetables were served raw. There were no rich gravies. There was no salt or sugar on the table. There were no alcoholic beverages, or after dinner coffee. There were no sweets served—only delicious fruits and nuts.

There was much laughter and conversation.

Death stalked the hallway, but for a short time the pleasure that prevailed at our unusual gathering prevented us from noticing.

When dinner was finished, a group of gospel singers came in from the local church. They sang beautifully, and with much feeling. There was a group of five: a young girl and boy of about Andy's age, two women, and an older man.

After the singing came to an end, one of the women in the group spoke to us.

She spoke in a strong voice that blocked out any rattling of silver or clinking of dishes from the kitchen.

"You have come far from your homes, but you have come closer to Christ. He has brought us all together, not as strangers, but as friends—to help each other. In all things, give thanks." She repeated, "In all things, give thanks, even for your suffering."

She asked us to stand and join hands.

We all stood, except for Doug, who couldn't. His hand reached out to Andy's which was clinging to his crutch. Andy unclasped several fingers to take Doug's hand. We formed a circle around them, joined hands, and prayed for the strength and recovery of all who were there.

Later there was a long distance call from home. Our family was gathered at Barbie's. There were brief messages, and shouts of "Happy Thanksgiving."

It was.

CHAPTER 11

The Very Important People

Legend has it that the Tower of Babel was a hospital. And as soon as all of the people scurrying about on the upper tower began speaking a language that no one else could understand, they were sent down to speak to the patients.

Since that misty prehistoric time, it has been the custom of the Hospital Land natives to speak in a strange tongue. They don't think their language is unusual: They certainly don't think that they are difficult to understand. In fact, they think they make perfect sense; It's you who are a little slow on the uptake. We know better, but we humor them because, after all, it is their island.

Charles Inlander
("Take this Book To The Hospital With You")

November 28, 1983:

The morning for our returning home had arrived. I had packed our belongings the night before. Andy had decided to leave most of his games with Abe. When Abe came in to say goodbye, he was very happy to accept them and had brought Andy a rock from the beach which Andy had asked for. Abe promised to write. Andy said, "Be sure you write in English, I'll never be able to read your 'chit-chat'."

Abe laughed. "Come back, Andy, when you're better. We'll go fishing."

Andy said, "You'll have to come to Owasippe."

They shook hands knowing that they would probably never meet again.

It was the custom of the clinic to provide breakfast for departing guests, and a small "doggie bag," so that they wouldn't have to start eating the processed food served on the planes. There were other patients also going home. We all had breakfast together and then were loaded onto the bus that would take us to the airport. Those left behind stood in front of the clinic calling out "good-byes," and wishes to "get well."

This time Andy did not have to be lifted onto the small plane. He was not in any pain and did not take any pain killers throughout the trip. (He hadn't needed them for at least a week and a half.)

We all waited together in the Antiqua airport. From this point on we would be flying in different directions.

When Andy noticed Doug lying down on the airport bench, trying to make himself comfortable, he walked over to him and gave him one of his pillows. Doug accepted the pillow gratefully, and put out his hand to Andy. He said to him, "Keep fighting, son, you' re going to make it."

Andy said, "So, are you, we' re both a lot better than when we first came here. Remember to drink your beet juice." (That was a standing joke among the patients.)

As we waited for our flight we watched the departures of the friends whom we had gotten to know so well in such a brief time. Then our plane arrived. Andy boarded it with ease and we settled back for our long flight to Miami.

When we checked into the Miami airport we knew we were back to reality. It was the weekend after Thanksgiving. The airport was jammed with travelers. Because this is a port of entry into the United States, it was necessary for the customs officials to open all of our luggage, (I was worried that they might confiscate the Laetrile which we

were carrying home—I had read of this being done).
Also we had only thirty minutes to make our
connection to Chicago. They were turning away
some passengers whose reservations were not
confirmed. I heard the girl at the ticket office telling
someone all the seats were taken. I was frantic
thinking we would be delayed in the airport
overnight. "We've just got to be on this plane,"
I told the ticket taker as she was about to close
reservations. Seeing our plight a couple in front
of us offered Andy and I their seats.

"Your plane is ready to take off," the girl at the
ticket window, told me. "But I'll call the pilot. There's
a chance that they will hold it for you."

The ticket taker called the pilot and he held the
plane. I ran—pushing Andy in the wheelchair—
all the way to the departure gate. We were the last
ones on the plane. Andy walked the long distance
down the aisle to a seat at the back of the plane,
something he could not possibly have done on our
way to Montserrat.

He turned down all offers of "Coke," sweets, or
any "forbidden" food. He was determined to stay on
his diet. He was in great spirits. We thought we had
won the battle.

We were met at the airport by Rita and her Mike—
little Mikey and Katie—Dave and Bern, John and
Mike—Barbie and Gabby—young Gabby and
Danny—Jeanne and her Glen—little Glen and Beth.

Andy walked off first. There were hugs and kisses and tears of joy. We were home!

Andy was better!

We continued the diet that they had used in Montserrat. There was only one health store where I could find unsprayed fruits and vegetables. I purchased everything I could there. I continued with the Laetrile in a tablet form as well as the numerous vitamins, minerals and enzymes.

Andy seemed to be doing well for a while. He was glad to be home with the family, and glad to be able to visit with friends.

He kept himself busy doing some writing, some paint by number pictures, reading books, playing games, and watching T.V. He even managed to attend a boy scout meeting.

It was his greatest desire to get well before camp time in July. Bob O'Hara, his scout master, had promised him that he would be "Camp Director." Bob visited Andy often to talk about their plans for camp.

But soon Andy was asking for a pain killer. Before long he needed two crutches to walk.

By Christmas of '83 Andy had to be carried into Barbie's.

We knew that the tumor was coming back.

It was on January 7, 1984 that we decided to take Andy into St. Luke's for more tests.

Andy was transported to St. Luke's in an ambulance. He joked with the driver and requested that they not turn on the siren.

"I'm not that sick," he told them.

John rode with him in the ambulance while Dave and Barbie and I followed. By the time we arrived at St. Luke's Andy was already in Room 1100. It was late and Andy was extremely tired.

The doctor was insisting on an immediate blood test. I objected to this because he had just had a complete test a few days previous to our arrival. I had brought the results into the hospital. I felt that Andy should not be disturbed that night any more than was absolutely necessary.

Dr. B. reprimanded me over the phone. He said, "We have some Very Important People coming here, and they never question my orders."

This information did not phase me even a little bit. I felt that Andy was as important as any other patient in the hospital, and that I was primarily interested in his comfort. I asked Dr. B. if he had ever heard of a "turkey" as referred to in the book called "Take This Book To the Hospital With You" (a book that I would certainly recommend to any person going into a hospital for any reason). He said he had not. I told him I would loan him my copy, and also that I planned on being a "turkey."

(A turkey according to the book, questions everything that is done to the patient).

This is done not to be a nuisance as it is regarded by the nurses and doctors, but to protect the patient from receiving any unnecessary tests, medication or treatments that might prove to be uncomfortable or harmful. It is the patient's legal right. I explained this to Dr. B.

He waited until morning for the blood test.

As I wanted Andy to remain on the diet he had in Montserrat, I prepared all of his food every night and brought it into the hospital every morning along with a bottle of distilled water. I also continued to give him the Laetrile and vitamins and minerals. There was no attempt to stop this, as I had anticipated, even though the nurses laughed at what they considered a useless effort on my part. But I was determined to continue the treatment that Dr. Manner had taught us, and Andy was certain that it was helping him.

Parking in St. Luke's parking lot is a real challenge. I would drive several miles through the winding labyrinth of cement columns and parked cars until I would find a space to squeeze the car into. Then I would carefully remove the boxes containing Andy's food and water and whatever else he had requested.

Struggling with these boxes I would search for the arrows pointing to the direction of the hospital.

Arrow four pointed to the long hallway which had an arrow pointing to the crowded elevator, which unloaded its passengers at the entrance of a winding glass enclosed bridge. The long bridge eventually ended in the main floor of the hospital. From there it was a trick to find the right elevator going up to Andy's room. There was a choice of elevator A, B or C.

As I searched for the right elevator, medical students, nurses and doctors, security men and other visitors hurried past me. Everyone moved swiftly through the maze of halls, their faces reflecting the fact that they were deep in thought. I guess mine did too.

And yet passing through all of the tunnels, crowding into several elevators and hurrying past the myriad of strange and solemn faces in this huge city of the sick, I would arrive in Andy's room to find his bright smile and cheerful greeting making it all worthwhile. He'd always assure me that everything was just fine.

Most of my visits were spent coaxing him to eat and take his vitamins.

The chemotherapy started a few nights after we were there. It was a very heavy dose of cytoxin, aureomyacin and vincrisstine. (I insisted on knowing exactly what it was.)

Andy was frightened at the thought of the poison going into him. He knew it was everything we didn't believe in. I was frightened too. I'll never forget the sight of the blue machine being rolled next to his bed and the needles being put into his frail arm. Rita and I stayed with him most of that night. He had no immediate reaction except a complete loss of appetite.

There were tests and X-rays—bone scans, and brain scans —pills—and more pills—blood transfusions, infusions and total confusion.

In between all of these tests Andy was constantly interrupted by medical students wanting to see or feel his "tumor," and asking hundreds of questions. I considered this an unnecessary intrusion on his privacy. Several times I asked them to leave.

It was very important to my job that I make a trip to Dallas, Texas. Andy seemed to be doing O.K. and I knew I would only be away for the weekend.

Eileen came in from Connecticut. Rose came from Great Bend, Kansas. They promised to take over my job of preparing food and visiting Andy every day. With them in control I had no qualms about leaving him.

Andy really enjoyed that time with his sisters. Living so far away it had been difficult for them to spend much time with him. They loved it too. Eileen said it was so great to become reacquainted with Andy. She and Rose played so many games with him. They did a good job with the food too. So the trip that I had dreaded taking turned out well for all of us.

While I was in Dallas with other vitamin salespeople, I learned of a better cancer treatment, which was administered at American International Hospital in Zion, Ill. I was informed that they gave Laetrile intravenously, and had a good nutritional program. I could hardly wait to get home and call them.

Soon after I arrived back home Dr. B. told me that Andy could be taken home from St. Luke's as an "outpatient" and brought in for chemo treatments.

Meanwhile I had contacted Dr. M. at American International. They would take Andy. They no longer were able to administer the Laetrile, however, due to restrictions of the AMA and FDA.

I told Dr. Bo we would be transferring Andy to American International rather than take him home. I had frequently explained to him that I wanted to keep Andy on the same nutritional diet that Dr. Manner had found so important. He had constantly scoffed at what he liked to call Manner's "quack" treatment. He wasn't interested in learning anything about it. He was too brilliant and educated to believe anything so simple as diet could affect the health of the body.

His arrogance and intolerable manner when I told him this news made me very happy that Andy was not going to be needing him any longer.

We called for an ambulance to transfer Andy to the hospital in Zion. The morning of our planned departure the phone rang at seven-thirty a.m. It was Dr. Bo.

He told me, "You will not be able to remove your son from the hospital this morning. He is running a fever. He could die on the way."

I replied, "Dr. Bo, I am taking Andy to a well equipped hospital in a well equipped ambulance."

He said, "I don't care where you take your son, he's going to die anyway."

I could not believe that this statement came from a doctor who had daily told me that his expensive and painful treatment was giving Andy a chance to live.

Dave, John and I went to pack Andy's things and take him to American International.

There was quite a delay in the arrival of the ambulance.

While we were waiting we asked at the desk for Andy's records. The intern on the floor told us he could not give out Andy's records. He put us through so much red tape that I had to contact the administrator and the chaplain. The intern told them that it was impossible to obtain the records until the next day.

Dave and John were busily packing Andy's belongings. He was totally unaware that all of this conflict was taking place in the corridor.

Then the ambulance arrived. The paramedics (a young man and woman) walked up to the desk on the floor and with an air of authority asked for Andy Reinert's records. The intern had them ready in about five minutes.

I was sure learning a great deal about hospital procedure. After obtaining the records, we left for Zion.

CHAPTER 12

More
Treatments

"He's not heavy. He's my brother."

Anonymous

We arrived at American International Hospital in the early evening about 4 p.m. It had taken all that time to transfer Andy, and his records from St. Luke's. After a short wait in the emergency room, Andy was taken to Room 309.

Dr M. explained to us that he wished to insert a catheter into Andy's shoulder. This would mean that all of his medication and tests could go through this catheter, instead of constantly sticking him with needles. This made sense. Andy was so tired of being stuck with needles. Also we had been told that prolonged use of needles could shrink his veins.

The insertion of the catheter required surgery and an anesthetic. When Andy was brought back to his room, he could barely move or even raise his arm to lift anything.

John said, "I can't stand to see Andy like this—I'm going to stay with him tonight."

I was so relieved. I had been wondering what we would do, as I had to take care of some things at home, and Dave had to get back to work. I had dreaded leaving Andy alone.

Then one night turned into another, and another— and it seemed that each day would bring a new crisis, so that John would be reluctant to leave. There was an empty bed in Andy's room, and also a large lounge chair. No one seemed to object to John staying over night. Actually by having John with Andy, the nurses were freed from a great deal of waiting on him, as Andy could not walk or sit up.

The doctors waited for Andy's fever to leave before starting any more treatment. They waited, too, for his white count to return to normal. The drop in the white blood count is something that occurs after every chemotherapy treatment.

Chemo drugs, such as Andy had been given (cytoxin, auoreomyacin, and vincristine) are deadly poisons. They do kill cancer cells. Unfortunately they also kill healthy cells, and break down the immune system.

American International attempts to build up the immune system while administering the dreaded chemo in lighter doses. They do this with large doses of Vitamin C, and an extremely nutritious diet. I still believe that if Andy had had lighter doses of chemotherapy in the beginning he might have recovered or at least not suffered all of the side effects that he did.

I dreaded seeing the "chemo" going in to him. I can still hear the "beep-beep" of the little blue machine that operated the I.V. pouring the poisonous drugs into his frail body.

After the chemo treatment, Andy always became very nauseated. He couldn't take any food. The trays that they brought in looked delicious, but Andy was unable to eat any of it. It became necessary to start feeding him intravenously. This also meant that it became almost impossible for him to swallow the Laetrile. How I wished that the AMA would permit its use here. It could have so easily been put through the I.V's.

Andy was just beginning to adjust himself to his new surroundings, when his beautiful black hair started falling out by the handful. This was a delayed reaction from the "chemo" given at St. Luke's.

There was hair all over the pillow. He asked for a shower cap to cover his head. He couldn't bear to have anyone see him. He asked me to bring dark pillow cases so that he wouldn't have to look at all the dark hair against the white pillow. His thick eyelashes, eyebrows and even his beard fell out. He was terribly upset. We assured him that it would grow back, even though we were uncertain ourselves.

Cards came by the hundreds. John taped them to the wall and soon the whole side of the room was covered. There were messages from his high school, from the family, friends, and even from strangers who had heard about Andy. There were humorous cards, serious cards, cards with love, and cards with prayers. Each day people let Andy know that they cared.

Andy's brothers and sisters made the long trip to Zion. It was 70 miles each way. But they came, and they came often. They left their families and their jobs to spend time with Andy.

Jeanne brought games and books. Rita made Andy's favorite pies with honey instead of sugar. Barbie made natural pizza. Dave brought fishing lures that Andy had asked for. Bernie came with his Bible and read long passages which Andy loved. And the family living in distant states didn't forget him either. Eileen sent daily letters and cards from her home in Connecticut. Rose wrote from Great Bend, Kansas. Carol wrote often from Houston, Texas. Tom called from Oregon.

His friends, too, made the long trip, bringing him news of their young world. He was so happy to see them. Sometimes there were so many in his room that the nurses could hardly squeeze past them. They never sent them away. They knew how much these visits meant to Andy.

They all laughed with him in his room but wept for him in the hospital hallways.

His boy scout troop—608—sent a singing telegram. A beautiful young girl walked into the room holding several dozen balloons and sang "Tomorrow" and "You're the Tops." John and Andy loved it. So did the nurses who gathered in Andy's room to enjoy the singing. John tied the balloons to the bar over Andy's bed. The cheerful balls of color remained there for weeks.

Everyone was trying to boost Andy's spirits. They did a great job of letting him know how much they cared. And John was Andy's biggest booster. He watched T.V. with him, encouraged him to eat, waited on him, helped with the physical therapy, ran to get the nurses when they didn't come fast enough—made him laugh through his tears.

He was Andy's legs, his peace of mind, the brightest part of his illness.

Andy clung to John. He needed him badly, and John never failed him.

CHAPTER 13

Hyperthermia

Oh for boyhood's painless play!
Sleep that wakes in laughing day,
Health that mocks the doctors' rules,
Knowledge never learned in schools.

J. C. Whittier (Barefoot Boy)

*T*here was a closeness of the patients and relatives at American International just as there had been in Montserrat, probably due to the fact that it was small and there were not too many patients, doctors—nor medical students. It wasn't like the big city atmosphere we had disliked at St. Luke's.

The patients had travelled from all over the United States. The majority of them had had a great deal of treatment, and were considered terminal. Many of them, like Andy, had been treated outside of the States or were considering it. They were ready to try anything. The odds weren't too much in their favor. But they were gambling with death.

The amazing phenomenon about all these suffering people was their ability to keep smiling and to freely discuss their illness, and hopes for recovery in spite of the odds.

What we didn't find out from the patients, we learned from their relatives. As we all spent so much time in the hospital, we usually ate together in the hospital cafeteria where we shared our experiences.

There had been much discussion about the hospital's hyperthermia treatment. American International is to my knowledge the only hospital that offered this treatment at that time. We kept hearing reports of its success.

The treatment consisted of raising the patient's body temperature to 107 degrees. Then the temperature was slowly lowered. The intense heat had the ability to shrink the tumor without harming the patient.

We spoke to Dr. M. about treatment for Andy. He explained to us that it was not always effective, but there were no adverse side effects. He felt that it was worth trying. So did we.

The cost sounded staggering—three thousand dollars. No insurance would cover this treatment. It was not considered of proven value by the AMA. I had pretty much gone through our savings with the trip to the West Indies. I would have to borrow the money. But where? I spoke to Jeanne and Rita. Without hesitation, they each wrote a check for fifteen hundred dollars. I realized that they were doing this at a great personal sacrifice. They were just starting out with young families, and there was no way of being certain when this could be paid back. They were willing to do anything to help Andy.

On the 29th of February, the nurses prepared Andy for the hyperthermia treatment. He looked frightened lying on the stretcher as John and I walked beside him to the door marked—surgery.

They had told us that he would be unconscious for 24 to 48 hours. Andy remained in the surgery room for about 30 hours. It was the evening of the following day when they took him to the intensive care room. There were tubes in his nose, tubes down his throat, tubes on his arm and in his shoulder, and the catheter which had become almost a permanent part of him.

The little blue machine was "beeping" at full blast. Andy didn't know what was happening. He was out cold. John and I remained with him.

As we waited through the long night with Andy, we observed the four other patients in the room. Their bodies looked almost lifeless, as the tubes and various machines kept them functioning. This was their last stop. As we watched them that night, I made up my mind that I would never allow Andy to be kept alive in this manner. There would be no "life-supports" to stretch out his last days. At least I could spare him that.

The following morning he was returned to his room. He was still extremely tired and slept through the day. When he woke up, he had no recollection of what had happened. He appeared to be in less pain.

Dr. M. said that the tumor had gone down somewhat. He suggested that Andy try to take less of the "diladin" pain killer that had been given to him at four hour intervals. Andy was a little afraid to go too long without a pain killer, but he agreed to try. The nurses withdrew the "diladin" completely.

A few nights later, Andy developed a talking streak that would not stop. John and I thought it was just a reaction from the hyperthermia. He was laughing one minute and crying the next.

Andy said, "Oh, it would be so great to play football. I'd love to run in a muddy field—remember John? Remember the fun we use to have playing football? I'd love to ride my bike, go fishing at Owasippe, or just to take a walk."

It was almost as though he wanted to be sure that these things had really happened to him—that there had been a time when he was healthy and could do things like everyone else. Andy had not walked without pain since September.

He wanted us to tell him stories about what he had done when he was well. I began to tell him some of his favorite stories about his early childhood:

I recalled the time when we were on a vacation at Sleepy Hollow. Sleepy Hollow is a family summer resort in South Haven, Michigan—right on the lake. There are acres of grounds to wander through. There is a large enclosed swimming pool which was out of bounds for the smaller children—unless accompanied by an adult.

Andy had been roaming around when he came to the porch where I was sitting and informed me about his new found friend. "Joe's only four and just dove off the high dive. I'm four, so I can go off the high dive." With that he ran to the pool. I was in hot pursuit but couldn't catch up to Andy. I arrived at the pool just in time to see him going off the diving board. Even though he could not swim, he had no fear. After he hit the water he just barely dog-paddled into his sister, (Rosie's) arms. Fortunately she was there.

———————

I reminded him of the morning, that I heard loud laughter over the noise of the vacuum, coming from his and John's room, Why, I wondered, were they running the vacuum at this early hour. It was 6:30 a.m. They were rarely awake at this time and certainly never concerned about the dust that was always attracted to their room.

I hollered above the noise, "What happened?"

I received the usual answer to the question that I have asked more than a thousand times, "Nothing."

But the noise of the vacuum and the laughter continued. Curiosity got the better of me. I had to get up and see for myself. As I opened their door, I couldn't see through the wall of feathers that confronted me. They had broken a feather pillow on the corner of the bed—while having a pillow fight. Andy was holding the vacuum hose in the air trying to suck in the thick cloud of feathers that enveloped the room. John was trying to stuff as many feathers as he could catch back into the pillow ticking.

Andy said, "Don't worry, Mom. We can make you another pillow. We're catching all the feathers in the vacuum."

———————

Andy remembered the night that our garage door wouldn't open. I called on him and John to help me so that I could get the car out to drive to the store. They managed to get the door raised just far enough for the car to pass through.

I was half-way to the store when I started to worry about the two of them in the garage. I thought of the possibility of the door coming down on them. I turned the car around and rushed home. When I pulled into the alley trying to park, I observed the door still closed with a note hanging on it.

The note read, "The door is completely broken. You will have to park in front." It was signed—Andy.

I didn't mind the door being broken. I was so glad to know that they had not been hurt. I still treasure that note.

———————

Andy laughed when I told him about the day when I looked out into the street and saw him in the middle of four or five scrapping dogs. I ran out in panic to rescue him. He wasn't one bit afraid. He was laughing and trying to pet them. He fought me as I picked him up, and the dogs scurried away. He said, "Mom, why did you make the dogs run away? We were having fun."

Another day, when he was almost five years old, Andy managed to climb into the driver's seat of our car and get it rolling out of the driveway and across the street...narrowly missing backing into a huge tree. I pulled him out of the car and gave him a whack on the bottom—probably the only time I had ever slapped him. He started to cry, and said, very indignantly..."I was driving."

This story always made Andy laugh: we had visited Rosie and her husband, Steve, one Sunday afternoon. It was one of those perfect June days. We played games and had a delightful backyard barbecue.

The highlight of the day was seeing the seven new puppies produced by Rose and Steve's loveable dog, Sunshine. Sunshine, who had always been so playful with Andy on our many other visits, was guarding her puppies with a ferocious motherly protectiveness. Andy tried repeatedly to pick up the puppies. Each time he was met with unfriendly growls by the new mother. Being only six years old, it was hard for Andy to understand the hostile attitude of his former playmate.

I could feel the disappointment in his voice, when he asked me, "Where did Sunshine get all those puppies, anyway?"

"Well," I told Andy, hoping the right words would come, "The father dog loved the mother dog and planted the seeds. Then God helped the seeds grow into puppies."

Andy's face brightened . He said hopefully, "Do you mean that we can buy 'puppy seeds'?"

I could never forget the day that Andy picked the heads off of Murphy's tulips—all twenty four of them. I can still see him running towards me, his hands full of the colored petals.

"I pulled flowers for you, Mom," he shouted eagerly.

Even though her flowers stood headless all of that summer, as a mute reminder of Andy's impulsive deed, Dorothy Murphy couldn't become angry with him. Neither could I.

There was the year of the big snow—1979—when Andy decided to buy a snow blower with his "life savings." Being the entrepreneur that he was he figured he could soon double his money shovelling

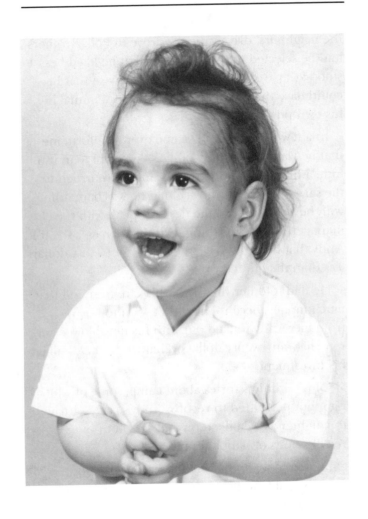

"I pulled flowers for you, Mom."

the neighbors' driveways. We drove to Polk Brothers and he selected the snow blower that he liked best. I stood away from him and the saleslady so that he could have the pleasure and experience of making his own purchase.

In a few minutes Andy came over to inform me that he was short twenty dollars—would I loan it to him? I handed him the twenty and he returned to the saleswoman. I could see that he was bargaining with her. She went to the desk to speak with the manager. After consulting with the manager she told Andy that he could have the blower at twenty dollars less than the quoted price.

He had told her that he didn't care to spend that much money, because he didn't want to borrow from me. Andy walked out with his new blower and returned my twenty dollars. That winter he doubled his investment.

John told him stories about camp, some of which I am not permitted to record. Andy's crying turned to laughter as we talked on and on about our recollections of happy times.

I hated to leave that night. It seemed good that Andy was able to let his feelings out. He and John were still laughing when I left for home.

When I got on the south-bound tollway to return home, however, I suddenly had a change of heart. I wanted to get back to the hospital early the next morning. Somewhere behind all Andy's conversation was a call for help.

I took the next exit on the tollway and decided to stay at Rita and Mike's for the night. They were only twenty minutes from the hospital and I knew their back door would be open even though it was late. They had invited me to stop whenever I didn't feel like making the long drive home. It was a good feeling to find Rita still awake and in her cheerful kitchen.

I didn't rest very well that night. I kept wishing that I had stayed with Andy.

I was up early the next morning, and arrived at the hospital about 8 a.m. When I reached Andy's room, John was almost in tears. Andy had been awake, and talking wildly all night. John hadn't been able to get help from any of the nurses or doctors. He had been awake with Andy the entire night.

The therapists were trying to take Andy to the whirlpool for his physical therapy, but Andy was refusing to go. He was almost out of his mind. The first thing that he said to me was, "Mom, I saw God last night. He told me that I'm going to get better, and that I'll walk again." He started to cry. I kissed him, and said, "Andy, that's wonderful. God will help you."

None of us will ever be sure whether he actually had a vision of the Lord, or whether he was hallucinating from the sudden drug withdrawal. I believe that it was the Lord's way of comforting him.

For four days and nights Andy kept talking. Very little of what he said made much sense.

He had one endless story of seeing three doors in heaven and how he was told to choose one to open. He would always choose one where God told him he would walk again.

There were many other stories too. It went on and on. His beautiful voice kept up this steady stream of tales that never happened.

Because it was the weekend we were unable to get any help for Andy. We were back and forth to the nurses' station trying to get help. They kept telling us that it was impossible to reach any of the doctors, so there would be nothing they could do until Monday. We were frantic. There was no way of knowing how long this condition would last, or if permanent damage had occurred.

I began to stay in the hospital at night also. There was no way that Andy could be left alone. He needed someone in the room every minute. There was an extra bed and a lounge chair in his room. John and I would take turns trying to sleep, but Andy talked without stopping. None of us could sleep.

When Monday arrived the doctors still did not visit Andy. They had a good deal of surgery to perform and even though we had asked for them many times, we were not able to see them until

Tuesday. The nurses were upset too. They knew Andy, and it was such a drastic change from his usually calm manner. Still nothing was done.

On Tuesday morning Dr. M. appeared. He told us that Andy's reaction was from the drug withdrawal of the "diladin." The withdrawl had been too abrupt. It should have been administered in smaller doses instead of being taken away completely. He instructed the nurse to give Andy "thorazine" (a mind drug) at four hour intervals. He assured us that Andy would soon be himself.

The nurse came in with a thorazine injection. She inserted the long needle into Andy's bony, aching hip. Andy hollered with pain. I immediately called Dr. M. to find out why this could not be given orally. "Wouldn't that be just as effective?" I inquired.

The next thorazine dosage was given in pill form. It worked just as well. (I cannot understand why hospitals are so needle happy. The comfort of a patient should certainly be put before the importance of using modern medical techniques.) It was that day that I promised Andy there would be no more unnecessary needles or tests.

It took three weeks before Andy was even the least coherent. I'm sure that many of his friends received calls that made them wonder about Andy's sanity. He would carry on hour long conversations with the wildest talk. The extent of his imagination came into full view at this time.

Dr. S. came in one morning and said they wanted to give Andy a brain scan. They had just given Andy a brain scan on Feb. 22. I refused. I also turned down any steroids that Dr. S wanted to give Andy. (I had seen what steroids had done to little Melissa in Montserrat).

I told Dr. S. that I wanted to wait for Andy's mind to clear before subjecting him to any stressful tests. That didn't go over real big with Dr. S., but I was much more concerned about Andy's feelings. His suffering was so great already, I didn't want him to have a mental problem.

Meanwhile Andy pulled out his shoulder catheter, and announced that he was going to eat. He was tired of being fed through a tube. He and John began going through the long menu and ordering all of their favorites. They had a delicious variety of food at American International and Andy began to enjoy it. He was eating everything on his plate with ravenous pleasure. He was even eating snacks in between meals. He had not been able to eat for two months.

Best of all he could now sit up in the wheelchair. John began to take him all over the hospital. He and John made the rounds to the rooms of all the patients. They caused a great deal of hilarity among the nurses, doctors, and patients, as they explored the parts of the building which Andy had never seen. Andy was greeting everyone as John, pushing him in his wheelchair, smiled his approval, delighted at Andy's new found freedom from Room 309. There wasn't a person in the hospital that wasn't familiar with the happy sight of the two of them touring the halls.

The doctors kept pressing for more X-rays. They had stacks of X-rays on every part of Andy's body. Again I told them that I felt we should wait for Andy's mind to clear.

Dr. M. told me that insurance would not pay for a person's stay in a hospital unless they were having tests made.

This did not seem like sufficient reason to me to subject Andy to more discomfort.

Dr. S. who had administered the anesthesia when Andy received the hyperthermia told us that Andy would die within a year, that this treatment only slowed the cancer for a short time. Dr. M. painted a picture of continued chemo, prolonged suffering, and the probability that Andy would die, (no way of knowing when). So who needs the torture treatment, I thought to myself.

There was much unrest among the relatives who were seeing their loved ones die, or wait for death as they were helplessly connected to life supports. We were all disappointed too in the large and strong doses of chemo that doctors from other hospitals were introducing at American International.

It began to occur to me that this might be a good time to build up Andy's immune system, and repeat the treatment that we had at Montserrat. Perhaps he could stay even longer this time. He had certainly shown improvement while he was there. If there was a chance to save him I knew this would be the only way.

We were hearing many good reports about clinics in Mexico with similar treatments to what Andy had had in the West Indies. The air fare to Tijuana was a great deal less than to the West Indies, which made it more within our reach. Money was a real problem. Insurance would not pay for treatment outside of the country. We did not have enough cash to finance such a trip.

And then like an answer to a prayer, Jeanne's friends started a benefit for Andy. Mary Martin, Ellen Norris, Karen Burke, Cathy Schmuel, and many others contacted Andy's friends in Christ The King Parish, and his boy scout troop—608. They knocked on doors, contacted business people. They spent hours on the telephone.

Betty Wadka, Larraine Weszely and many others encouraged the students at Evergreen Park High School to conduct bake sales, raffles, and special dances. The response of the students was overwhelming.

Through Maureen Dombro, and others, Holy Redeemer Parish and even local grammar schools made generous contributions.

There was a benefit dance at Christ the King School Hall. Hundreds of young friends of Andy's and the family attended. Without hesitation they opened up their hearts, and dug deep into their pockets to raise money to help with Andy's soaring medical bills.

It would be impossible to name each generous person who contributed, but we will always remember their generosity and kindness. Without their help many of the things that we were able to do for Andy would have been impossible.

Shortly after the benefit John and I met Mary Martin at Concordia Bank. Mary was carrying the huge bag of money and checks collected at the benefit concealed under her coat. She had attached it to a string around her neck. She laughed as she told us that people glancing at the huge bulge must have thought that she was pregnant.

John and I sat down with her at the bank. She said she and her family had counted out the money the night before. They had collected over ten thousand dollars! Mary told us that we could spend the money for Andy in any way that we thought he would benefit.

I couldn't think of a better way to use it.

Andy could have another chance!

We could take him to Mexico for more Laetrile!

CHAPTER 14

The Search Goes On

Forth than issued Hiawatha
Wandered eastward,
Wandered westward.
Teaching men the use of simples
And the antidotes for poisons,
And the cure of all diseases.

Longfellow 1855

*A*pril, 1984:
    Barbie and Gabby picked us up at the
hospital in his mother's van and drove us directly
to O'Hare Airport.

We boarded our plane at 10:30 p.m.—destination
San Diego, where we would be driven over the
border to the G. clinic in Tijuana.

I knew it wouldn't be as easy for Andy to travel
this time. His condition was far worse than it had
been on our first trip. He had to be lifted from the
wheelchair to the narrow carrier that enabled him to
be rolled down the aisle of the plane. Then John
would carefully take his legs and the steward would
hold him under the arms to lift him into his seat.

Also we needed to carry so many things. We
brought three pillows to make Andy comfortable. He
sat on one, his feet were on another and he had one
between his legs to support their weight. (He had lost
almost all control of his legs.) We had made sure that
we would each have sufficient clothing in case of
another loss of luggage, so that entailed carrying
quite a bit of baggage with us.

The trip would have been impossible without
John. Besides being such a great help, his sense of

humor made laughable many situations which might have otherwise been annoying.

The flight to San Diego was smooth and uneventful. It was a night flight and there were only about six other passengers besides Andy, John and myself. It was almost like having our own private plane.

We arrived in San Diego at twelve thirty a.m. We were met at the airport by a cab driver who was familiar with the location of the clinic. He spoke very little English. Andy was tired and it was difficult for the driver and John to lift him into the cab without hurting him.

When we arrived at the clinic we were extremely disappointed. The whole place was filthy and uncared for. There was no T.V.—no phone—no air conditioning—not even a fan. The only window (which had no curtain) looked into the hallway where everyone passing by could look into the room.

No one spoke English except for the few patients that were there. There was one interpreter I finally learned, who was available between ten and twelve in the morning. (Why didn't I listen to my mother and learn some Spanish?)

The following morning there were conferences and information as to what they planned to do. Their methods were very similar to the treatment at Montserrat, but the dismal atmosphere was beginning to depress the three of us.

We walked Andy around in the wheelchair. Even that was difficult. There was very little sidewalk and what there was was cracked so badly that it was difficult to maneuver the wheelchair without jolting Andy.

At about five o'clock that day after eating an extremely unpalatable supper, and looking at John's and Andy's unhappy expressions, I decided that we would leave for Montserrat.

Without telling them what I was doing, I walked the block or more to the office, which contained the only telephone. After more than an hour of total exasperation and complete frustration, I was able to locate an English speaking operator. I made reservations to fly to Montserrat the next morning.

Returning to John and Andy I told them the news. Andy grinned and said, "Wonderful, let's get out of here."

John put his arm around me and said, "That's the best decision you ever made. This place is crummy."

We were ready the following morning at four-thirty a.m. The same cab driver took us to the San Diego airport. He was a little surprised at our swift departure, but he did his job and got us to the plane on time.

We landed in Denver. It was cold and we were unboarded outside. They placed Andy (wheelchair and all) onto a stair carrier and pushed him to a ramp going into the airport. A stewardess stayed with him. She wrapped a blanket around his shoulders. He was laughing and waving as John and I tried to keep up with the fast moving carrier.

The stewardess stayed with us until we reached the gate leading to our plane to Miami. Before she left us, Andy pulled out a five dollar bill and insisted that she take it for her unusual service. She didn't want to, but she couldn't say no to Andy.

We went on to Miami where again we were faced with confusion and crowds at the airport. John by this time was a "seasoned traveller" and had taken over the job of checking our luggage, and the details necessary to leave the country.

After boarding our plane to Antiqua we were told that we would have a 45 minute wait—something in the plane's mechanism needed adjusting.

As the waiting period grew longer, we were informed that we could leave the plane, but only to go into the locked waiting room, otherwise our hand luggage would have to be examined again. I walked out to see if it was possible to take Andy in there, but it was so crowded and full of smoke, that I knew he would be more comfortable remaining on the plane.

He was also beginning to be very nervous from the long delay. We didn't want his nerves jangled, because we knew his "drug reaction" was still not completely cured.

We waited for five hours. After that we were transferred to another air line. Because of the

154

delay we would be missing the once a day flight to Montserrat. The stewardess informed us that anyone missing a connecting flight would be bedded and fed at the Antiqua Inn. After our long delay we were glad for the short stop in Antiqua.

The following morning we were flown into Montserrat.

It was just as we had left it—a beautiful paradise. John was delighted at the sight of the pool and the nearby ocean. Andy was glad to be back. The whole place was such a contrast to the clinic in Tijuana.

The nurses could hardly believe how much Andy had deteriorated in such a short time—only four months. I believe that the extremely heavy doses of chemotherapy had done him more harm than anything else.

The treatment began again. Andy was not as cooperative. His mind still wasn't completely cleared from the reaction to the drug withdrawl. John got him out to the pool every day, but he could only sit and watch. There was so little mobility in his legs that had grown so pitifully thin. Yvonne, the physical therapist couldn't do much either, as any pressure on the nerves created too much pain.

After we had been there for almost a week, John and I were called into a conference with Dr. Manner, Dr. Cooper and the head nurse. I knew when we walked into the room that whatever they were going to say was not going to be good. Their expressions were grim. They told us that the tests showed that the cancer had spread. Andy's liver was not functioning properly. Also the cancer had entered his spine. Much of his pelvic area was destroyed and his entire sacrum was eaten away.

There was nothing more that they could do for him. We were advised to take him home and let him spend his last days there, as Andy spoke over and over of wanting to be with his brothers and sisters. There was no way of knowing how long he would live—possibly six months.

Now I believed it. Andy was going to die. There was no more that we could do. John and I cried. We had had every hope that we would be able to save him. We had travelled thousands of miles searching for a cure, spent endless days and nights watching him fight through his suffering. The search was over. We were going to lose Andy. There was nothing we could do now but return home.

Andy was glad to hear we were going home. We didn't want to tell him the reason just yet. He didn't ask any questions. Perhaps it was because he was still suffering from his bad drug reaction.

It was with heavy hearts that we made our preparations to depart....

Andy loved the travelling. (I will always be glad that we had that trip together. He enjoyed meeting so many people and the excitement of flying.) And having John with us made it a fun trip in spite of the suffering that we were all experiencing.

We remained in the Miami Airport motel overnight, thus avoiding the terrible rushing that we had to do on our last trip to make our connection. John and Andy had a good time playing all the video games in the arcade, and looking through the shops.

Andy was taking pictures of everyone who would pause long enough to pose for him. And John as usual was spurring him on. People were touched and amused at Andy's friendliness. The sight of his smiling face even though he was confined to a wheelchair caused many people to stop to speak with him.

We flew home the next morning, and were met at O'Hare by Barbie. It was a much more solemn home coming than our last one. Although nothing was said, the family knew now that Andy had no chance to live.

CHAPTER 15

There's No Place Like Home

Mid pleasures and palace, over land, sea and foam,
Wherever we wander, there's no place like home.

John Payne

B ack Home (Late April and May, 1984):
Andy was so glad to be home. He had spent
three months in hospitals. Dave and Rita had
ordered a hospital bed for him and contacted a
nursing service. Linda was our first nurse. She
became everyone's favorite—especially Andy's. She
knew how to talk with him, and showed a personal
interest in everything that he did. Also she made
very little reference to his illness, and yet she would
answer any of his questions with honesty.

They both liked to listen to the country singer,
Willy Nelson. Linda would bring her tapes and play
them while she was taking care of Andy.

She told him amusing stories about her family.
She listened to his stories, and laughed at his
jokes. When listening to Andy, John, and Linda,
I sometimes found it hard to believe that Andy
was so ill.

Andy wanted to be with people and to be
outdoors as much as possible. It was getting warm
enough so that he could enjoy being outside. He
might suddenly say, "Let's go down to the White
Hen." Dave and John would help him into the
wheelchair and away they'd go.

Jeanne invited him to view some of his favorite movies on her VCR. John, Dave and Mike carried Andy (seated in his heavy wheelchair) up three flights of steep stairs to view the movies. It was a strenuous trip for all of them and even worse when they carried him back down. He didn't ask to visit Jeanne's again. He knew that it was too much of a strain on everyone to carry him up those steep stairs.

He decided that he would like to take a trip to the zoo on Mother's day. He invited his brothers and sisters and their families to go along. They all agreed that it would be great fun. They hadn't been to the zoo in a long time, and they were all aware of Andy's love for animals.

The zoo trip was disappointing. It was a windy cold day. It was difficult to get in and out of places of interest. Being a holiday it was overcrowded. Small children ran into the wheelchair, causing Andy a great deal of pain, unless someone walked in front of it. Before long, Andy said, "Let's go home." More and more he was beginning to feel his limitations. However, he was still determined to keep from being totally confined. Shortly after the trip to the zoo, Andy picked up the phone to seek information from the staff at the Shedd Aquarium. He wanted to know whether they had ramps to accommodate his wheelchair. He inquired as to the exact location of the ramps, and about admission charges. He asked for information concerning recreation for handicapped people. (I always marvelled at Andy's directness when he spoke with anyone. He had such a straightforward way about him. He would come to the point in a very few words. I believe that Andy would not have hesitated to call the Pope or the President, if he wanted information from them. And I am equally sure that they would have found it a delightful experience to talk with him.)

He was ready to try another outing. He informed us that Thursday was a free day at the Aquarium, and that he would like to go. We all set out together. It was a little more pleasant than the trip to the zoo. But again, being in a wheelchair prevented him from seeing many exciting exhibits at close range.

We spent a short time in the souvenir shop and Andy purchased a few items. I watched while he bought things which I knew he would never use. Somehow it didn't matter. We so badly wanted to see him having a good time.

We could see that the trip was only making him more aware of his condition. We hadn't been there long when Andy suggested leaving for home.

Shortly after we arrived home, Barbie called to ask Andy to stay with them for a few days. Andy was eager to go. He wrote about his visit in the following chapter.

CHAPTER 16

Graduation
June 8, 1984

His life was gentle,
and the elements so mixed in him
That nature might
Stand up and say,
This was a man!

William Shakespeare—1599

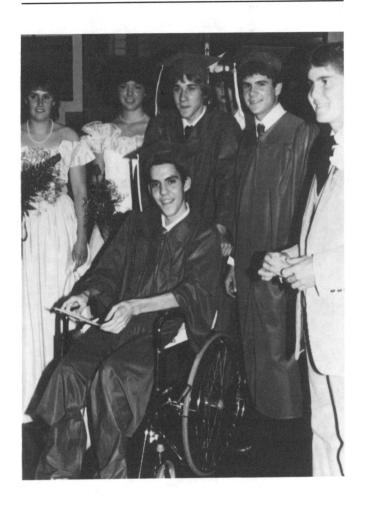

Tom Fritz and Rene Mlot pushed me down the aisle.
I had graduated from Evergreen Park High School.

*J*ust after Memorial Day I went to stay at my sister Barbie's for a few days. I love to be at Barb's. She's across the street from a large schoolyard, where we played ball all the time. I could watch my friends from the living room. Barb fixed a bed for me right in front of the window so that I could see them. Every night she builds a fire in the fireplace, and my friends come over to play games with me.

They are all talking about graduation, girls, college, cars, and jobs. All I wish is that I could walk and get better. They are so lucky, and don't even know it. It isn't fair.

It's getting close to my graduation, and I don't know if I can really face it. I hate to be different and I hate to have everyone looking at me...in a wheelchair.

I don't know if I really earned a diploma. I haven't been able to study that much. Dr. Renfrow, the school administrator, called and said to do what I wanted. My Mom did too. They both said to think about it.

Tonight there is a graduation party for Bobby Whalen, and I'm going. Bob and I have been friends since kindergarten. He's super. I'm going, but I'm afraid. I haven't been out much with my friends since I've been sick, except to go to a boy scout meeting.

That night I came home and cried. I cried because I was handicapped. I could no longer walk among them and be myself. The younger kids stared at me. A few even made hurting remarks— I am afraid to go tonight, but I must. I want to be with my friends.

AFTER BOB's PARTY

I did it. I went to Bob's party. My brothers—Bernie, and John—and our friend, Joe, helped me in and out of the wheelchair. They wheeled me into the Whalen's yard. I looked at the crowd—they were laughing and dancing. I felt so out of it.

One of my friends came over to me, and I started to cry. Bob's mother and father must have understood, because they came running out of the house to talk to me. I felt better then, and was able to have a fairly good time with my friends. But it was lonely.

When I got home, I told my Mom—"Now, I can go to my graduation, I know what it will be like."

Last night I graduated from Evergreen Park High School. John helped me to get dressed...It takes so long to do everything—hours just to take a bath. I use to be in and out of the shower in about five minutes.

I'm sure glad my hair has grown back. It looked great. The school sent over my cap and gown. I was glad I had decided to go. I did want to graduate with my class.

Rene Mlot and Tom Fritz came to the house to escort me. They looked so good. They are true friends.

I was finally ready. Dave and John lifted me into the wheelchair. The graduation gown covered the catheter (I don't think I'll ever get that thing off).

They wheeled me out to the car. It hurt when they lifted me into the back seat. Things that use to seem so simple have become so hard to do.

We pulled up right in front of school. There was a crowd standing around. I felt like everyone was staring at me when they lifted me out. I waved and smiled to some of the kids I recognized and some of them came over to talk to me. That made me feel good—like I belonged.

This was my class. These were the kids I had grown up with, studied and laughed with. They have done a lot for me. They have really shown that they care about me. But I'm different now. I can't walk and do the things they do. They couldn't possibly understand.

Tom and Rene pushed me down the aisle and placed me next to the bleacher seats.

The music started.

I sat and watched my classmates walking down the aisle. I felt like crying, but I didn't. I didn't want anyone to see me acting like a baby.

The ceremony seemed so long. I did like the singing, and the talks. At last they started to hand out the diplomas. I thought they would never get to the R's.

My leg was beginning to hurt, even though Mom had given me extra pain killers. They were calling my name—"Andy Reinert."

They had built a special ramp going up to the stage just for me. Imagine that! As Rene and Tom pushed me up the ramp, everyone stood up and clapped and cheered. All the teachers on the stage shook my hand. Someone handed me my diploma. I had graduated from high school. By that time my leg was killing me. I asked Rene and Tom to push me right out of the hall. They did.

John was waiting in the back for me. He congratulated me and took over. I feel better when John's around.

We stayed in the hall where we could still look in at the graduates. They threw their hats into the air.

John asked me if I wanted to throw mine.

I said, "No, I want to take it home."

A mother remembers:

It was after Bob's party that Andy was able to make up his mind to attend the graduation ceremony.

Just to get him into the bathtub was hard on him and very time consuming. It took John about two hours to help him wash, shave, and dress. It was impossible to rush Andy since his illness. Each movement was such an effort. Any sudden jolt would bring on more pain. And of course Andy stalled.

He'd keep saying "later" or "wait a minute," as he bargained for more time. John made him laugh at his clumsiness.

Dave and John helped him into his new white shirt and blue tie. Pants had been a problem, as Andy's waist had shrunk from 32 inches to 18 inches. It was difficult to pull pants over his legs without hurting him. We had to settle for some with zippers on the sides. Andy made no complaints.

Rene and Tom arrived with the green graduation cap and gown. They had come to escort Andy to school. The students and faculty had thought of everything to make it easier and more pleasant for him.

When he was finally ready, he looked better and happier than I had seen him looking in a long time. After he was carefully maneuvered into the wheelchair, he smiled and said, "Come on, let's go. We don't want to be late for graduation." He said it as though we had been keeping him waiting, instead of the other way around.

Knowing that the ceremony would be an emotional and physical strain on Andy, I had not expected the evening to be a happy one. It had been a tough year for Andy. There had been no parties and proms, no football games, no final exams, no last day of school. It had been a pain filled year of needles, X-rays, pills, doctors, hospitals, and endless tests—all the things that should have been unknown to a boy of seventeen—certainly a poor substitute for the joys of being a senior in high school.

But as always, Andy set the pattern. In spite of his anguish and pain, he carried off the night in his unselfish style. He did it with acceptance, courage, and yes even with laughter.

Somewhere between that first trip to the hospital and his graduation night, Andy had matured from a fun-loving boy to an extremely courageous young man.

He had more than earned his diploma.

CHAPTER 17

Summer of '84

And does it not seem hard to you,
When all the sky is clear and blue,
And I should like so much to play,
To have to go to bed by day?

Robert Louis Stevenson

A ndy had received a new typewriter from the family as a graduation gift. He spent hours every day typing letters and recording his thoughts and feelings. We also rented a computer. The high school sent over a very competent young student, Jeff Witt, to give Andy some basic instructions to operate it.

Much as he enjoyed these diversions, his pleasure was short lived. It was becoming increasingly difficult for him to sit up for very long at a time. Gradually he was unable to lift his legs back onto the bed from the floor. John would have to carefully lift his legs as Andy slowly lowered himself to a comfortable position. Even raising one end of his bed put too much of a strain on his spine. Now he was lying down most of the time.

About this time Dave Hollander and Bob Klier brought Andy a VCR. They had held a drive to procure the necessary funds to purchase this wonderful gift. They brought it in as a complete surprise to Andy...They connected it for him, and promised that any films he wanted would be provided at the local video store without charge. The VCR probably meant more to Andy than any other gift he had received. Long hours of entertainment from the movies gave him a great deal of pleasure and kept his mind happily occupied.

He and John would spend time going through the lists of movies. Then John would make his weekly trip for the desired films. Andy liked us to sit with him to watch the movies. To share them was much better than watching alone. Often he and John would be up until two or three in the morning talking and laughing at their selected shows.

In August, Andy went into a coma. We were told that this could be the end. It was during this time that our friends, Maureen Dombro and Mary Jo Allison, suggested having a Mass at home.

We notified the family, and prepared for Father's arrival—to celebrate Mass in our home.

That was our first meeting with Father Mike. Maureen and Mary Jo joined us. We stood around Andy's bed and prayed with Father. Andy slept through the Mass, but was able to take Communion. Later that day he surprised us by coming out of the coma. Perhaps that time was given to him to become acquainted with Father Mike.

At first we thought of Father as just a priest, performing his duty. But it didn't take many visits, before Andy was eagerly awaiting his arrival.

Andy wrote about Father:

Father Mike is coming today. I love to have him visit us. He brings Communion and we talk for a

long time. He never seems to be in a hurry. John and
I always try to have some new jokes to tell him, and
he always has some for us. He brought us a tape
from the church musical. In it he did an imitation of
Tiny Tim. We were all cracking up when we watched
it. I couldn't stop laughing. Father seems more like
a friend than a priest. He's just a regular guy. He
doesn't talk much about God, but I feel closer to
God when he's around.

Father came often to visit Andy after their first
meeting. They offered each other a renewal of
faith as their friendship grew with each of Father's
precious visits. Andy saw God more clearly through
Father Mike, and Father saw Him more clearly
through Andy.

The warm summer days passed slowly for Andy.
He could hear the loud laughter and happy
hollering from the nearby pool. He could see the
joggers running by, and the children playing in the
sunshine. He watched the bikes ride past during the
day, and the endless stream of the headlights of
passing cars, carrying their unseen passengers,
lighting up the night.

Andy, without complaint, watched through the
window...as summer passed him by.

September 7th was Andy's eighteenth birthday. The day before he had kept his cordless phone busy reminding his brothers and sisters and friends that he would like to see them. Andy had always reminded people of his birthday, so it was not especially unusual. He had always considered his birthday an event of extreme importance and never had allowed it to be overlooked.

He never hesitated to ask favors of people and they never failed to grant them. He was a person who made others feel as though he was doing them a favor by asking a favor of them.

Everyone whom he called assured Andy that they would see him on his birthday.

They did not disappoint him. He had many visitors—a few at a time. The family and grandchildren came in—presenting their gifts— their happy faces masking their aching hearts. All day and all evening friends came to wish Andy "Happy Birthday" for the last time. Some seemed a little hesitant about how they were going to handle the awkwardness of such a tragic situation. He would simply put out his hand to them, smile his big grin and put them at ease.

They went away, feeling glad that they had come.

CHAPTER 18

I Love The Rain

Tears, idle tears, I know
not what they mean.
Tears from the depths of some divine despair
Rise in the heart and gather to the eyes.
In looking on the happy Autumn fields,
And thinking of the days that are no more.

Alfred Tennyson

*M*om finally told me that I am going to die. I guess I have known it all the time, but I just couldn't talk about it.

I asked her tonight if there wasn't something else we could do. She sat down on the chair next to my bed, and took my hand. She said, "Andy, the doctors have all agreed that there is no more we can do to save your life. I can only tell you that the worst pain is over, and we will still do everything we can think of to find a cure."

"Will they have to take my leg off?" I asked her.

"No," she said, "no way, you'll be right here with us...no more hospitals, no more tests, no more needles."

I don't know why, but I feel relieved. Now I know I won't have to lie here forever like this, and I can talk about dying.

But when I looked at my Mom, I felt bad. She was trying not to cry. I wanted to say something to cheer her up. So I said, "I don't mind dying, Mom, but I know that you're going to feel so bad."

She didn't say anything—just squeezed my hand a little bit tighter.

I wanted to make her laugh. I asked her, "Do they have fishing in heaven?"

She did smile at that.

"They have everything in heaven, Andy."

"Then would you put my fishing pole in with me?"

She said she would.

We both cried for a while, and so did my brothers. I hate to leave everyone. We have such a great family.

I am sure though that I will be in heaven. I looked at them and said, "We will all be together again in heaven. But, Mom, you still have some improving to do. Remember what we said?"

She did laugh then, and so did Dave, Mike, John and me.

It's raining hard tonight. I asked John to open the curtains so that I could watch it. It's such a good feeling to be inside when it's pouring rain outside. I love to hear the thunder and see the lightning.

It reminds me of a lot of things I did when I could walk—like the day I went on the walkathon in my yellow raincoat. It really poured on us. We kept walking until my legs and feet were sore. My raincoat was soaked on the inside and my feet were blistered. But we had a ball. What I wouldn't give to be able to walk like that now!

"Is there fishing in heaven?"

I especially remember nights and days at Camp Owasippe when it rained. We would be running in and out of the tents. We couldn't do much then, except play some card games, read books, sing camp songs, and tell ghost stories.

We'd be drying out our clothes for days. I'd love to see camp just once more. I use to think I'd get back, but now I know I never will. I wonder what kind of scout camps they have in heaven. They must be filled with 'good scouts' (ha-ha).

I remember one night when I was in fifth grade. Mike Gricus stayed over night. It rained so hard that the streets were flooded. The whole street in front of our house was like a river. It was up to our knees. We actually saw two rabbits swimming around. We waded all over the street trying to catch them. Mike and I always had fun together.

The rain especially reminds me of a song our family use to sing. They told me they learned it from their first grade teacher—Sister Honorata. These are the words:

> I love the rain, when the rain is raining,
> I love the rain, raining down on me.
> I love the wind, when the wind is blowing,
> I love the wind, when it's blowing me.
> I love the snow, when the snow is falling,
> I love the snow, when it falls on me.
> I love the sun, when the sun is shining,
> I love the sun, when it shines on me.

Mom said that the verse means more than just loving the weather. She said that it means loving the tough times in our lives and making the best of them, just like we do the good times. She always said that good things came even from hard times.

I know now what she meant. There are some good things about my cancer. Everyone has been so great to me. I realize how much they care about me. I've gotten to know the whole family a lot better. They do so many things for me. Dave washes my hair and shaves me. He rubs the back of my neck when it's sore. It hurts so much some times, because I can hardly move my head now. I have to grab the top of my hair and pull my head up just to get a pillow under it.

And John is unbelievable! He stayed home from college to help me. He stays with me all of the time, and does a million things for me. We talk a lot late at night. He's so much fun to have around. He keeps me laughing even when I'm afraid.

I appreciate more the things that I am able to do. I can still read and write. My eyes are still good—and so is my mind. I was really flaky from those drugs for a while. That was a weird feeling. I couldn't stop talking. Glad I can think straight now.

It's strange too that I should feel closer to God now that I am suffering so much. Bernie helped me to understand by explaining some things in the Bible to me.

I have had plenty of time to think about Him. I know that I will see Him soon! I'm not afraid to die. I'm afraid of the pain.

No one knows how long it will be before I die—so I will just try to do whatever I can for each day that I am here.

I'm afraid of the pain —
but I love the rain!

(The start of a great new poem by Andy Reinert—To be completed—Tomorrow?)

CHAPTER 19

Christmas, 1984

There's a song in the air!
There's a star in the sky
There's a mother's deep prayer
And a baby's low cry.
And the star raineth fire,
While the people sing.
For the manger of Bethlehem
Cradles a King.

*A*s Christmas grew close, we weren't sure just what to expect. We remembered that Thanksgiving of '84 had been too confusing and emotional for Andy. He had finally asked everyone to leave. He just couldn't take the noise and merriment. They all understood, but Andy felt that he had spoiled everyone's holiday by sending them home. We were concerned that Christmas would turn out the same.

But Andy had other ideas. He insisted that we purchase gifts from him for everyone in the family. He wrote long lists and sent each of us on shopping trips. He inspected our purchases carefully when we brought them home. If they didn't come up to his specifications, he would simply ask us to exchange them for something that did. When he was completely satisfied that the gift would please the person for whom it was purchased, he would carefully wrap it, and store it in the box which we had been instructed to place near his bed. Even though we offered our help, he insisted on wrapping every gift himself. This was in spite of the fact that he had to lie flat on his back, and hold the gifts and wrappings over his head.

Cards started arriving. Oh kind and thoughtful people—what those cards meant to Andy!

His friends from Evergreen Park High School led by Tom Fritz and Rene Mlot, came in with boxes of food, brightly wrapped gifts, hundreds of cards with cheering messages, and an envelope with money in it.

Their young faces showed their concern and sorrow at the obvious physical change in Andy's appearance. He soon put them at ease, questioning them on what they were doing. Their laughter and boyish conversation was great medicine for Andy. He always loved people and excitement. He was indeed happy...But Andy was no longer "one of them". They spoke of the future; Andy could only live in the past.

We placed the tree at the foot of Andy's bed. It was a natural tree. The fragrant aroma of the pungent pine penetrated the room. It diminished the offensive odors of medicine, and other foul smells, which are cancer's constant companions.

For many years, Dave had assigned himself the job of putting the lights on the tree. He began his task, while Andy gave orders as to where to switch the bulbs around so that too many of one color would not appear in the same area.

Dave smiled as he carried out Andy's commands. We were always delighted at the way he wanted to be a part of everything that was happening. Giving instructions was Andy's only way to participate.

When the lights had been satisfactorily arranged, Mike (assisted by two of the grandchildren—Glenn and Danny) began to unwrap the crib figures. Our replica of the Nativity had been a gift from the three oldest children—(Tom, Eileen, and Carol) one Christmas long past. The little figures distinctly showed their years of fond handling, and unfortunate accidents, which all too frequently take place in a large family. The donkey was missing one leg and had to be propped against the stable wall. (Every year we promised him a new leg, but somehow he got back into the dark Christmas box and put aside until the following December without the promised leg.) One wise man had lost part of his crown; Mary's veil was a little chipped; St. Joseph had only one ear; and baby Jesus had a bruise on His nose.

And yet, as Mike placed each of the battered statues, wearing their colorful garments, into their position of adoration, they brought to mind that First Christmas.

Bernie, whose Bible is one of the few items he never loses, read from it the passage on The Birth of Jesus:

> *"AND Joseph went from Gallilee out of the town of Nazareth into Judea to the town of David, which is called Bethlehem—because he was of the house and family of David—to register, together with Mary his espoused wife, who was with child. And it came to pass while they were there, that the days for her to be delivered were fulfilled. And*

she brought forth her first born son, and wrapped Him in swaddling clothes, and laid Him in a manger, because there was no room for them in the inn. And there were shepherds in the same district living in the fields and keeping watch over their flock by night. And behold, an angel of the Lord stood by them and the glory of God shone round about them, and they feared exceedingly. And the angel said to them, 'Do not be afraid, for behold, I bring you good news of great joy, which shall be to all the people; for today in the town of Bethlehem a Saviour has been born to you, who is Christ the Lord. And this shall be a sign to you: you will find an infant wrapped in swaddling clothes and lying in a manger'."

As the ornaments began to appear out from under their wrappings, the misty memories of past Christmas celebrations were brought into sharp focus.

Andy recalled the year 1976. He was ten years old. He received his first two-wheel bike. Barbie and Gabby had kept it hidden. They wheeled it into the living room after all the other gifts had been distributed. Andy was so excited and happy that he had to rush out, with no concern for the below zero weather, to ride it twice around the block.

There was the year, 1957, that we had a new slide in the dining room. We had miraculously encountered two gentlemen removing it to the warehouse— to make room for the fairy like Christmas display of toys that at that time occupied the entire fourth floor of Marshall Field's State St. store. We bargained with them, and couldn't believe it was ours for an unbelievably low price. Needless to say it was a big hit.

The sight of a little goldfish ornament reminded Rita of Christmas, 1964. She and Mike had requested an aquarium. To their delight the desired aquarium was bubbling away on Christmas morning. It contained three tropical swordfish, which were all we were able to purchase with our limited budget.

Before the day was ended, fifty-two baby swordfish were born into their world of water, while Rita and Mike watched with wonder and amazement. Rita counted them as they made their unexpected appearance.

She exclaimed, "Oh, are we lucky. We have fifty-two baby fish."

Barbie standing close by, sounded the alarm— as only she could do. With great excitement she hollered, "Holy mattress— these fish are prejudiced."

The sight of an angel wearing a sequined skirt transforms Jeanne back to a little girl of twelve.

She had asked for a white dress. "I can wear it for Easter, Christmas, and graduation," she rationalized.

The "white dress" was the last package she unwrapped. After carefully removing her dress from the box, Jeanne stood up and held it against herself. We could feel her joy and satisfaction when she hollered, "I got it. I got it. I got my white dress!"

The sight of a little soldier and Barbie was four again, standing on the stairs in her red flannel nightgown. She had broken our Christmas rule of waiting to open the packages until we were all awake.

Her eagerness to see her things could not wait. She had been up during the night and opened each of her gifts. She looked as though she was going to cry. Guilt was written all over her little face. But her Dad soon picked her up and had her laughing about her daring deed.

It was 1979—the year of the "big snow" and the bitter winds, and the high gas bills (which forced everyone to keep the thermostat as low as possible). Andy presented me with a bright yellow electric blanket. He had placed a little clown on top of the package. The blanket's electric coils have long since lost their heat, but the clown still warms my heart, as he smiles at us each Christmas.

When Andy instructed Rosie to move the little felt boy with the fishing pole closer to his bed, he started to laugh as he thought of Christmas, 1980. None of us can forget the expression on John's face, nor his roaring laughter, as he ripped the paper off of a very significant gift—a reproduction of a Norman Rockwell Saturday Evening Post cover. The illustration showed three naked young boys—running with their clothes over their arms—a sign in the background reading in large letters—"NO SWIMMING". Evidently John didn't want to hear this story. He placed a record on the stereo.

Our voices were soon faded out, as the words of "Come All Ye Faithful" filled the room. Andy started to sing along with the record. One by one we sang along with him. No one in our family has ever been noted for possessing an unusual talent for singing, but no chorus could have sounded more melodious to me than the combination of their voices proclaiming their love for the Blessed Life born in Bethlehem almost 2000 years ago, and Andy leading them with a voice so strong, that it belied the weak condition of his pain-filled body.

There would be no need to have an ornament to remember this Christmas. It would live in our hearts forever. It was a Christmas filled with pain, unexplained joy and—love. And love is eternal. It is stronger than pain, stronger than cancer, and stronger than death itself.

We could feel that love. We could hold on to it. We could be happy because of it.

Later, when everyone had left and I kissed Andy good-night, he took my hand and said—"Didn't we have a fun Christmas, Mom?"

CHAPTER 20

Whatever
It Takes

"This is the true joy in life,
the being used for a purpose recognized by yourself
As a mighty one."

George Bernard Shaw

*T*he Christmas tree remained at the foot of Andy's bed until almost the end of January. Each time that I would begin to remove it Andy would plead, "Leave it up a few more days." It wasn't hard to persuade me. Somehow we all wanted to hang onto that Christmas.

But the needles were falling fast. The tree became so bedraggled looking that Andy said one morning, "You'd better get rid of the tree. It could start a fire."

A great deal of Andy's strength seemed to leave him along with the Christmas tree. He could no longer be turned without terrible pain. It was impossible for Nurse Linda, John and myself to turn him from his back to either side. And it was essential that we turn him frequently to clean the bedding and to bathe him. Also lying in the same position was causing ugly raw sores to form on his back. These had to be treated and bandaged.

We had started to think about putting him into a hospital when Carol Lacoscio, a neighbor, suggested that we call the Evergreen Park Paramedics to help us.

When we called them, they came at once. They were a sight for weary eyes. They arrived wearing their spotless uniforms, an understanding of suffering, and their professional efficient techniques. They won our hearts and confidence immediately. They moved Andy from his bed to their carrier. Nurse Linda cleaned the bed and we were able to place an air mattress on it to make him more comfortable. As capable as they were, it was John who directed them as to just where they could touch Andy without hurting him. They kindly cooperated and gently moved Andy with as little pain as possible. It was necessary to give him gas. Andy objected to this the first time, but asked for it many times at subsequent visits.

The wonderful paramedics told us not to hesitate to call on them. They had been aware of Andy's condition, and offered their assistance whenever we thought it necessary. We called on them many times after that. They always arrived within ten minutes of our calls.

Andy was now not only confined to bed, but was forced to lie in the same position twenty-four hours a day. He could not turn to his side without the help of the paramedics. He spent all day and all night on his back, with his legs propped on pillows. His knees were pulled up—he could not straighten his legs or move his feet. He had to grab the trapeze over his bed to raise his head even the slightest. In order to eat, we had to place a towel over his chest and place his plate on top of him. He drank all liquids through a straw.

In spite of all this discomfort, he never showed any sign of depression or complained about the long hours that he had to lie there. Occasionally I would see tears trickling from the corners of Andy's eyes. When I'd ask softly if he were crying, he'd answer, "No, my eyes are just watering a little." He did not want anyone to see him cry—mostly because he did not want anyone else to suffer. His consideration for others was remarkable. I'd have to turn my head so he wouldn't see my tears. He couldn't bear to see me cry.

Now that Andy could no longer turn over, it was difficult for him to see anyone sitting behind his bed. We had arranged the bed in the living room where he could have the best view of the outdoors. The furniture had been arranged around him so that everyone in the room could see the T.V.

He rigged up a mirror, so that he didn't miss anything going on behind him. He also managed to see everything happening in the kitchen through the reflection in the patio doors. Andy wanted to be a part of everything going on. He knew when I had turned the stove burner too high, or if I was struggling to open a jar (he had often done that for me with ease—now his hands had become too weak). Several times he had asked me to bring the frustrating jar to him—only to find himself equally frustrated and hand it over to Dave or John.

Many times Andy would send John or myself back into the kitchen because his food was too hot or too cold, or maybe the butter wasn't evened off on the toast just the way he wanted it. He'd ask for more ice in his water, or that the fan should be turned on or off.

We welcomed every suggestion. There was never any impatience or reluctance in granting his requests. His pleasures were so few. It was so good to have him ask for anything.

Also Andy had always been a leader, in spite of his position of number twelve in the family line-up. We knew how important it was for him to give orders—especially now in his helpless condition. This was an essential part of retaining his dignity, and possibly his sanity. It was the only way he could be a part of our daily activities.

I watched John with amazement, doing the wash, bathing Andy, emptying the catheter, waiting on Andy, watching goofy movies with him and pretending he loved them, sleeping on an uncomfortable couch next to Andy's bed—night after night, jumping up at Andy's least call, massaging his legs, preparing food, changing sheets, but more than anything banishing his fears, carrying on lighthearted conversations, making him laugh through his suffering, and showing Andy how much he was loved.

If I have said that Andy never complained, I could only say the same about John. John had given up school, his freedom to come and go as he pleased, every waking hour, as well as much of his sleep at night to care for his brother.

Frequently I worried about him giving so much of himself and all of his time.

When I would tell him this he would simply say, "I'm not going anywhere. I could never leave Andy now. I'll be here until the end...whenever it happens...whatever it takes."

CHAPTER 21

"So Long Scrappy"

Wee sleekit timourous cowrin' beastie,
Oh, what a panic in thy breastie,
Thou neen na start awa' sae hasty
Wi' bickering brattle!
I wad be laith to run and chase thee
Wi' murdering prattle.

Robert Burns 1785

*A*ndy was cheerful most of the time. He did dread the paramedics visits, as moving him from side to side was extremely painful It was such a slow process. John would take his legs while the paramedics would hold his torso, and they would roll him over ever so slowly. But no matter how slowly they tried to move him, Andy would say "go slower." The whole process of cleaning him, and changing his bed and bandages would take over two hours.

We could always tell when Andy was getting the effects of the gas, which he held over his face himself. He would remove the mask and start questioning the paramedics on their activities. They replied with stories of recent accidents, trips they were planning, sports news, and anything they thought would be of interest to Andy. He put the mask back over his face when the pains became unbearable again. Even though he dreaded their visits because of the pain that being moved caused him, he grew very fond of each of them. He never failed to thank them when they were leaving, and apologize for giving them a hard time.

Andy's pain killer seemed to be losing its effectiveness. Lying on his back in one position, his legs unable to move, was giving him severe muscle cramps in his legs and hips. It would seem to come over him in the middle of the night. He would scream out in pain. By the time I would reach his side, John would be gently massaging his legs.

One night we called the paramedics five times to administer the gas that he had at first rejected. They came without complaint to help Andy.

It was the suggestion of one of the paramedics that we should change Andy's medication or start using I.V.'s or needles. I knew Andy did not want any more needles, and I had promised him that we would stay away from the I.V.'s. To have his arm restricted by them on top of his other problems would have just made him that much more miserable.

We were lucky in finding Dr. Baron, a local oncologist, to come to our aid in prescribing a stronger pain killer.

Andy liked Dr. Baron immediately. Baron had a compassion for his patients which was so lacking in most of the doctors we had had. He also had a good sense of humor, which Andy loved.

Andy never wanted to be treated any differently than he had been treated when he was well. He still had the mind and spirit of a young boy in spite of his illness and suffering.

As Dr. Baron left after that first visit, Andy asked the question that we knew was always on his mind.

"Dr. Baron, do you think I'll ever walk again?"

Dr. Baron, even though he knew Andy was dying said, "Andy, give me a chance. This is only my first visit. We' re going to work at it."

I liked what he said and the way that he said it. Even though we had told Andy he was dying, I don't believe that he ever fully accepted it as a certainty. Fortunately his great determination and unusual positive attitude plus his strong faith kept hope in his heart until the very end.

Not only did he keep hoping, but there were days when we would really believe that he was showing improvement. He was always so amazingly cheerful. The medication had put an end to the muscle spasms. There were no longer any screams at night. He was taking morphine in a tablet form. It was not necessary to give him any needles. I was glad of this, as Andy had such a fear of them.

Andy was always a great talker. When he wasn't talking with us he would spend time on the phone with his sisters, brothers and friends. As I have mentioned before Andy was great to talk with. He never lost this ability. His voice was strong and pleasant, and full of enthusiasm. He rarely spoke about his illness.

In between conversations Andy kept himself busy. I never heard him say, "There's nothing to do." He always found things to do, and was extremely interested in what every one was doing.

He was a collector of many things. Two of his favorites were beer cans and money. Dave had placed shelves all around his room to display his collection of beer cans. If he received new ones he would instruct John or Dave as to where they should be placed.

He kept a record of his bank account, and would send us to the bank to make deposits for him, always keeping a record of the transaction. We made a habit of emptying our change into cigar boxes every day for Andy to count. He'd diligently wrap the coins in their proper wrappers and save them until he felt that it was time for them to be taken to the bank.

John had given him The Tolkien stories as a birthday gift. Andy spent hours reading them. As they were paperbacks it was easy to hold them even though he was flat on his back. He would frequently send us to the dictionary or the world books to find the meaning of some word or phrase which he might not understand.

Something in one of the Tolkien books reminded Andy of the hamsters he had once had as pets.

One day he said, "Mom, do you think we could get some hamsters?"

"What a great idea, Andy. I think I know someone that has a few too many." (I never thought that I could be so happy over the prospect of having hamsters.)

A friend had just made the announcement that her son's hamster had recently fathered eleven little offspring. Hearing that Andy wanted them, she immediately sent her son Steve to bring four of them to him. Andy was pleased, and started planning additions to the rather crowded cage that Steve had so generously given him for the hamsters.

He made out a list and sent Dave and John to the pet store. They soon returned with a maze of plastic tunnels, turning wheels, wood shavings, and hamster food. The high school sent over an extra cage. The living room began to look like a pet shop. The hamsters put on quite an act for Andy. They ran through their tunnels and around their wheels in a steady frenzy of activity. John fell heir to the job of cleaning their quarters and feeding them, so he didn't share Andy's enthusiasm, but to see him watching them with Andy, anyone would believe that he would rather be watching hamsters than doing anything else.

Occasionally one would escape the cage. Then we would conduct quite a hunt for the wandering animal—much to the amusement of Andy and John. (They were doubly amused at me hunting for it because they knew that I was afraid of them and couldn't pick one up if I found it).

One night, after an endless search did not reveal the whereabouts of Scrappy (the largest of the group) John and Andy devised a plan to get him back into the cage. John placed the food into the cage, crumbled newspaper in front of the entrance which he kept open, and put a small lite nearby. They would wait for the approach of the hamster (which usually occurred around three in the morning). When they would hear Scrappy running noisily across the paper, John would quickly leap off of the couch, swing the cage door down and outwit the hungry little animal. I always knew when Scrappy was in the cage again, when I heard them laughing loudly. I'd find myself laughing, too, even though it was the middle of the night. It was so good to hear the sounds of laughter instead of the screams of pain.

This game went on for a number of nights. I suspect that the two of them freed Scrappy just for the fun of recapturing him.

Andy awoke one morning to find that two of the hamsters had died. A few days later another one was dead. This bothered him a great deal. He called the local pet store to find out whether they would take the last lonely little creature. He was afraid it would die also. The pet store told him that they had an over supply of hamsters and they did not want to introduce a strange hamster to their existing families. They suggested trying to find someone who liked animals.

Andy turned to John and asked him to find a home for Scrappy. John happily consented. He packed up Scrappy and his belongings in a very short time.

As John departed with the cages and the hamster, Andy said, "John, don't just leave him anywhere. I don't want him to have to suffer." It was typical of how he felt about every living thing—even this tiny animal.

John replied, "Don't worry, Andy, I'll take good care of Scrappy.

"I'm sure you will, John."

They both laughed and Andy said,

"So long, Scrappy."

CHAPTER 22

Miracle on 88th Street

Don't lose sight of your spirituality. Believe me my
friends, it is all you have.
All the rest means nothing.
All your strength, all your brains, all your
achievements, your honors...nothing really matters.
And remember, when we suffer, and above all
when we suffer as HE suffered, helpless and held back,
we may be at the highest point of
our lives...not the lowest.

(These words were given to Andy by a dear friend—Betty Hansen).
Author unknown

*J*une 30th, 1985:

Andy took a turn for the worse. The paramedics came in to move him. The mattress needed cleaning, so they had to lift him off of the bed. John and the three paramedics used the sheet as a stretcher to place him on their carrier, while Nurse Linda changed and cleaned the bedding.

We had given him large doses of morphine to prepare him for the dreaded visit of the paramedics, but after being lifted he was in excruciating pain.

He cried out in agony, "Oh, God, where are you? Did You take a vacation?"

The paramedics, Linda, John and I could do nothing for him. We stood in tearful silence, as Andy screamed in pain.

Fortunately, he fell asleep from the effects of the morphine, while on the stretcher. Lifting him back onto his bed didn't bother him.

He slept through the rest of the day and night and part of the following morning—almost 36 hours. We had seen him like this so many times after the paramedics came in—but this time his drowziness seemed to be lasting longer.

July 1:

Andy would wake up occasionally and speak to us. He was coherent when he spoke but his voice was weak. He complained that his throat was hurting— so I gave him some aloe vera juice, which always seemed to help.

Rita and her husband Mike had come to visit us. I had planned a chicken dinner, hoping to tempt Andy's appetite, as he always liked something special after the paramedics' visits.

Andy had apparently been still asleep, but when he heard me say we were going to eat, he opened his eyes and said he was hungry. When I had prepared his plate, he appeared too weak to feed himself. (He had always managed to do this. He never liked to have anyone feed him). I tried to give him a spoonful of potatoes and gravy. He took a small portion on his tongue and told me to take it away.

Andy slept most of the time during the next few days. His eyes were half-open. Only the white portions were visible.

We kept trying to spoon water into him. He took very little, and no solid food. He was not in a coma. When he was awake, he spoke very softly, but clearly.

July 4th:

Andy seemed a little bit more awake today, still very weak and quiet. He had been planning to shoot off fireworks—or rather having Gabby and John do it. They had purchased a number of firecrackers,

and were ready to entertain Andy, as soon as it
got dark.

Andy told us that he didn't want to hear the
noise of the fireworks. As it grew dark we could see
the display in the park from our window. Andy
requested that the curtains be drawn.

"I don't want to watch any fireworks," he said
almost in a whisper. This was the first holiday that
Andy had no desire to take part in.

He dozed on and off the rest of the week—eating
and drinking very little.

July 11th:

Andy's voice had become so weak that we could
hardly make out what he was saying. He asked
for watermelon.

"I'll have to run to the store for some, Andy. I'll get
it quick, and be right back."

He said, "Hurry, go now, hurry."

There was such an urgency in his voice. Was it
thirst or knowing that his time had almost run out?
As I sped to the store, I prayed that he wouldn't die
before I got back home...I wanted to be with him.
He was asleep when I returned from the store. He
didn't get his watermelon. He slept most of the day.

Father Mike came in. It was such a comfort to have
him there. He remained with us for a time. Andy
seemed to know he was there. Father rubbed his arm
and Andy responded with a smile, but didn't speak.

After Father left, John and I stayed close to Andy. He seemed disturbed if we left the room.

His head was turned to the right. He was resting on the ear with the sore spot that we had tried to heal for so long. His legs were propped on pillows unable to move at Andy's will. His arms were dreadfully thin and bony. Every rib in his young body stood out prominently. His beautiful eyes were so sunken that his cheek bones had an almost skeleton like appearance. His skin was taking on a greyish cast. I knew he couldn't possibly live much longer....

That night Andy was choking up a little. He seemed to be having a hard time swallowing. He asked Dave to give him 'mouth to mouth'. They had all been in scouts so many years, that Dave knew just what to do. Andy was relieved a little when Dave finished.

In a weak whisper Andy said, "I know I'm dying, Dave."

Dave gently took his hand, and said, "Andy, do you believe you will be in heaven?"

"I know I will," Andy replied.

Then he requested that Dave read to him from the revelations. (Andy's always wanted plenty of information when he was planning a trip).

Dave read from his Bible—"You shall walk again with the Lord."

Andy asked him to repeat this line. Dave read the words over several times. Andy smiled—it had been almost two years since he had walked normally.

He slept through the night. John stayed on the couch near to him as he had done so faithfully during his illness.

Several times, I got up to check if he needed anything. Once he asked me to "straighten his head." I put my hands on either side of his face and tried to turn his head from the right side. I couldn't. I was terrified. I couldn't move his head—nor could Andy.

July 12th:

Andy was still sleeping when I woke up—still with his eyes half open. He was breathing normally—we always watched his chest to see if it was still moving up and down—so many times expecting his breathing to stop. He woke up at about eleven o'clock. He asked for "watermelon" again. This time I had it ready. I had cut some into very small pieces for him. He took a few little bites and then said, "No more."

He asked me to place his arms on the trapeze. It was with great effort that he was able to lift his arm—even with my help. I had to place my hand over his to keep his arm from falling.

He kept saying, "Push my arm."

I didn't know what he meant. John jumped up and slowly pushed the trapeze sideways. (John always seemed to understand exactly what Andy wanted).

His arms were so weak. They slipped off of the trapeze and fell back to the bed.

"I can't raise my arms," he whispered.

I sat by the side of his bed, holding his hand. He seemed to want me there. Then suddenly he took his hand away and clasped both hands together over his chest. He appeared to be saying a prayer.

He took four gasping breaths. I heard a little gurgling noise from his throat. I saw his chest stop going up and down.

Andy was dead.

It was Friday—twenty minutes past noon.

———

The intensity of Andy's suffering and the manner in which he suffered bore a similarity to the suffering and death of Jesus Christ. This thought occured to me, as I later prayed before a crucifix.

Christ's head was turned to the right, so was Andy's.

Christ's back was raw with open sores from rubbing against the hard wood of his cross.

Andy's back was raw and sore from the constant pressure of ten months of lying in the same position in his bed.

Christ's arms were nailed to the cross.

Andy, too, was unable to move his arms.

Christ's feet were nailed and unable to move.

Andy could not move his legs, or even wiggle his toes.

Christ's chest was bare.

So was Andy's.

Christ said, "I thirst."

Andy asked for watermelon.

Christ called out, "Father, why have you forsaken me?"

Andy asked, "God where are you? Did You take a vacation?"

Christ turned to the thief on the cross and said, "This day you shall be with me in Paradise."

Andy told his family, "We'll all be together again in heaven."

So Andy suffered and died in a Christ-like manner. So have many others. This was not the miracle.

The miracle was the courageous way in which he suffered and died...It was the way that he accepted each long hour of his suffering. It was the way that he felt about others, and succeeded even in his worst pain in considering the feelings of everyone.

It was not any big thing that he did. It was all the little things that he did in such a big way.

It was his ability to live each painfilled day with faith, love and laughter—to keep faith in God, to continue to love life and everyone around him, and to look death in the eye with a smile on his face.

This unusual courage is what gave so much beauty and meaning to the untimely death of such a vibrant young man.

This was the MIRACLE that happened on 88th Street.

CHAPTER 23

Gone
Fishing

I devise to boys jointly all the idle fields and commons where ball may be played—pleasant waters where one may swim, all snow-clad hills where one may coast and all streams and ponds where one may fish or when winter comes one may skate, to have and to hold the same for the period of their boyhood, and all the meadows, with the clover blossoms and the butterflies thereof—the woods, the birds and squirrels and echoes and strange noises and all distant places which may be visited together with the adventure to be found.

Charles Lounsbury (last will and testament)
1872

*T*he first thing that John and I did after Andy's death was to put our arms around each other and thank God that his suffering was at an end. We had kept him at home where he had wanted to be. For that we were very happy. His suffering was over. The realization of our own would come later. But now there were many things to be done.

One of the first people I called was Bob O'Hara— our long time friend and neighbor, and Andy's scout master. Bob was preparing to drive to Camp Owasippe. It was Troop 608's last day at camp. Bob was driving up to help them pack and return home. He was saddened at the news, and said he would let the scouts know.

Bob drove for four hours that afternoon. He thought of Andy as he made the long trip. They had been good friends, and had had many good times together. He liked Andy's sense of humor and outstanding leadership qualities. He was glad that he had visited Andy often during his illness. He would miss him.

It was just getting dark when he arrived at Camp Hiawatha Beach in Whitehall, Michigan. He turned up the tree-lined road that he had driven with Andy so many times. His car made it up the sandy hill that wove a curved path into the camp that Andy had so loved. He didn't know just how he would tell the scouts. They were all glad to see Bob. They had just started their dinner. He sat down with them and some of the fathers who were there.

After dinner he took a ride around the lake, just before packing up the canoes. It seemed like such a short time ago that he had done this with Andy.

The boys were building a fire as Bob pulled his canoe into shore. They sat together on the logs around the fire—on the edge of Big Blue Lake. They sang a few camp songs and talked about going home.

Someone said, "How's Andy?"

Bob broke the news, "Andy died today. He died peacefully, and he died at home."

There was silence and tears. Then they prayed together for their lost friend—the scouts that he loved—sitting together in his favorite place around the camp fire on the edge of Big Blue Lake.

The scouts arrived home the next day in time for the wake and funeral. Bob had thought of everything. The boy scout flag was at the head of Andy's casket. The scouts were all wearing their uniforms and badges. (How they managed to appear so immaculate, after two weeks at Owasippe, I will never know.) There was a long line of young faces scrubbed and suntan—so solemn at the sight of death. I had never seen them looking more magnificent.

The funeral was a beautiful tribute to Andy's brief life. It was held at Holy Redeemer Church. Our friend Gus Du Bois led the choir with the beautiful as well as appropriate song "I'll Raise You Up On Eagle Wings."

Father Mike spoke with obvious love and feeling of the friendship that had meant so much to him and to Andy. At the end of his eulogy, he held up a card which Andy and John had given Father on his birthday. It read—"You're a very special person— one of God's better ideas."

His voice quivered a little as he attributed the same qualities to Andy. He said emphatically, "Andy is—not 'was' (for Andy still lives with Christ) a very special person—one of God's better ideas."

Father Mike asked the pallbearers—Andy's brothers, Mike, Dave, Bernie, and John, Gabbie (Barb's husband) and Bob, along with the family to stand around Andy's casket as he gave him a final blessing. Father included young Gabby, Danny and Glen in the ceremony by permitting them to sprinkle Andy's casket with holy water.

As we walked down the aisle and out of the church behind Andy's casket, the grandchildren held on tightly to the metal box, as though they did not want to let go of their "favorite uncle" (a title which Andy had always insisted on being called).

Mike Heeney, the funeral director, gently removed their tiny hands as the huge box containing Andy's body was lifted into the hearse. Through my tears I could see his much loved boy scout troop standing in long lines in the back of the church.

The final parting came as we watched his casket being lowered into the ground.

Danny, overwhelmed by this awesome moment, asked with faith and concern, "Grandma, has Andy got his fishing pole?"

CHAPTER 24

Andy Walks Again

*They looked...and behold the glory of the
Lord appeared in the cloud.*

(Exod. 16:10)

I had to return to American International Hospital today—two months after Andy's death. The hospital is so small that you can see the whole building from the parking lot. I parked where I usually had when I visited Andy so that he could see me from his window. I could almost see his smiling face there.

I could feel a chill going through me, just as I always had felt when I approached the hospital, always fearing some dreaded news.

I walked into the building and up to the emergency room. I could picture Andy everywhere. I could see him there on the rolling cart, where he had waited in the emergency room. He was in every wheelchair that went by in the halls. There he was in the surgery room, where John and I had waited while Andy had his hyperthermia treatment. I walked past the intensive care room. He was lying there unconscious, with all kinds of hoses going in and out of him, and the machines monitoring his body functions.

I went up to Room 309. There was someone else in Andy's bed now. I said "hello" to the very sweet lady lying there. But even while I talked with her, I saw Andy in that bed—where he had spent two months with his hopes and fears.

I turned to leave. Funny the girl at the desk did not even recognize me—or was she a new girl? I wasn't sure.

As I walked down the stairs Dr. Melijor was walking up. He knew. We talked for a short time.

"You tried so hard to save him," I said.

"Yes, we tried. He was a wonderful boy. You'll need time to forget."

I surprised myself by kissing him on the cheek. He had been Andy's favorite doctor, in spite of our differences of opinion.

I walked out of the hospital. I crossed the street. There is a beautiful little park there. In the center is a duck pond—well inhabited. There were many mothers and their children in the park. There was a little baby with dark hair, sitting placidly in his buggy.

I thought of Andy as a baby, his beautiful curly dark hair his big brown eyes, framed with exceptionally long thick lashes, his adorable smile.

I could see him crawling across the floor and whistling. It was a strange but precocious habit that he had as an infant.

I could see him running towards me—his hands full of a neighbor's tulips, his heart full of love.

I saw him driving a hard bargain when he decided to purchase his own snow blower. I saw him riding

his bike, fishing and swimming, diving and skiing—
always laughing.

I saw him standing straight and tall as I pinned
his Eagle Badge on to his shirt. How proud we
both were!

I saw him on his Graduation night being pushed
up the ramp in his green cap and gown.

I saw him on his last Christmas, determined to
make us happy.

I thought of the beautiful tenderness that had
grown between Andy and his brothers and sisters. I
thought of the very special love that had grown
between John and Andy—his last days that were of
such bittersweet beauty and simplicity. There was a
constant exchange of spontaneous conversations,
requests that were immediately granted, and love
and pain that showed in the eyes of these two
brothers—one wanting so badly to live, but having
the courage to die—the other giving so much love
and laughter, while his own heart was breaking from
watching his brother suffer.

I thought of Father Mike who had given us so
much strength, who had brought Andy and all of us
closer to Christ, with his gentle ways, his compassion
and caring, his unfailing sense of humor, and the
generous giving of his time.

I saw Andy clasp his hands over his chest and take
his last breath.

I saw him in his casket dressed in his boy scout uniform that he loved (the first time that he had had clothes on for months). The green graduation cap was in the corner by his head—he was taking it "home". The requested fishing pole was at his side. His pain was over.

Cancer had destroyed his body. But nothing could destroy his spirit.

It was getting late. The children and their mothers were gone. Even the ducks were deserting the pond, huddling their feathered bodies together in preparation for the night.

The air had grown chilly. I slipped my jacket on, and as I prepared to leave, I glanced at the sky. There was a magnificent formation of clouds. The greys and blacks were edged with silver brilliance. The sun, only partially visible, pierced through the dark clouds in perfectly spaced diagonal rays that appeared almost to be touching the far end of the pond.

It was a glorious sight, and gazing at it with awe, I could feel the presence of God.

And then I knew. I knew without any doubt. I will see Andy again! I'll see him walking!

For Andy, at long last, is walking with the Lord!

So live, that sinking in thy last
long sleep
Calm thou mayst smile,
While all around thee weep.

William Jones (from the Persian 1775)